KU-520-084

Christmas

Christmas

BLANDFORD PRESS, POOLE, DORSET.

First published in 1978 by
Blandford Press Ltd.,
Link House,
West Street,
Poole, Dorset.
BH15 1LL.

ISBN 0 7137 0 846 8

© 1978 Blandford Press Ltd.

All Rights Reserved, including the right to
reproduce this book, or parts thereof, in any
form, including microfilm or other audio-visual methods..

Devised by Terence Goldsmith
Editing and Picture Research: Jacqueline Ridley
Design and Layout: John Clark
Original Art Work by William Cameron Johnson,
  David Dowland and Joyce Smith
Original Photography by David Couling

CENTRAL STOCKS UNIT
TAMWORTH ROAD
HERTFORD SG13 7DG
TEL: 586 863

HERTFORDSHIRE
COUNTY LIBRARY
J394.268
9223334

26 JUN 1979

0.7G P

Printed and bound in Great Britain
by Purnell & Sons Ltd., Paulton (Bristol).

Contents

ACKNOWLEDGMENTS

CHRISTMAS has been conceived as a whole but has been compiled in parts. The publishers are most appreciative of the distinguished contributions to this anthology from each of the specialist authors whose acknowledgment below, rather than with the section they have written, is intentional in order to preserve the unity of the overall Christmas theme.

Contributors

The First Christmas
- Adapted from the Gospels of Luke and Matthew
Christmas Around the World   **REGINALD HOLME**
Music   **ARTHUR HUTCHINGS**
Paintings   **JAMES HAMILTON**
Crafts   **PAMELA WOODS**
Cards   **MICHAEL RIDLEY**
Saints   **DOROTHY PRESCOTT**
Cooking   **JACQUELINE RIDLEY**

in association with the Dept. of Catering, Bournemouth College of Technology

Stories for Christmas
Hole in the Sock   **ALAN THORNHILL**
Baboushka   **DAVID COULING**
The Christmas Dinner of Silas Squeer   **HANNEN FOSS**

Particular thanks are due to the British Library for making available for photography the world famous Bedford Book of Hours from which *The First Christmas* has been designed. *Christmas Around the World* was compiled by Reginald Holme from accounts given to him from correspondents in many parts of the world, to each of whom he would like to express his thanks. Thanks are also due to the Director, Chefs and Students of the Department of Catering of Bournemouth College of Technology for their special preparation of all food photographed for *Cooking*. The illustrations for *Baboushka* are by 11-year-old Caroline Mallett, winner of the special *Baboushka* children's competition organised by the *Bournemouth Evening Echo* and the publishers. The publishers would like to record their indebtedness to the large number of people without whose wholehearted support and co-operation this book could not have been published, but due to lack of space individual acknowledgment has not been possible.

The British Library - 8-21; Netherland National Tourist Office - 22; Will Green - 24 top; Camera Press - 24 bot. (David Rubinger), 65 (B. G. Silberstein); Bryan Alexander - 26; Finnish Tourist Board - 3; Mary Evans Picture Library - 31, 40, 42, 47, 48, 56; Irish Tourist Board - 32 (Paddy Tutty), 33; Photo Library International - 34, 62 (Clint Clemans); Radio Times Hulton Picture Library - 35, 37, 39, 45, 119, 122; Dept. of the Environment, U.K. - 38; British Tourist Authority - 42; Navosti Press Agency - 46; U.S.P.G. - 49, 51, 53, 54, 63, 66; Dr. R. K. McAll - 'Poo Tung Pete' - 52; John Clark - 57; William Cameron Johnson - 59, 69, 70, 71, 72, 73, 75 (reproduced from The Golden Book of Carols), 132, 136, 141, 145, 147; David Dowland and Joyce Smith - 27, 28, 43, 60, 152, 153, 155, 159; Origination Photo Library - 64, 109, 112, 114, 120, 125; Prado, Madrid - 76/77, 90/92; Fitzwilliam Museum, Cambridge, U.K. - 79; Tate Gallery, London U.K. - 81; Pinakothek Gallery, Munich - 83; San Marco, Florence - 85; National Gallery of Art, Washington - 86/87; Stadtbibliothek, Trier, Fed. Rep. of Germany - 88; National Gallery, London - 89; Birmingham City Museum and Art Gallery, U.K. - 92; Uffizi Gallery, Florence - 93; Italian Tourist Board - 93; David Couling - 94/95, 96, 101; Valerie M. Monahan - 108, 112, 114; Victoria and Albert Museum, London - Renier Coll - 116; Caroline Mallett - 148, 151

Preface

From time immemorial mankind has made merry 'in the bleak mid-winter'. In the Western Hemisphere at least, a time of feasting and festivity has marked the shortest days and longest nights of the year when the seasons are turning from the barrenness of winter towards the rebirth of nature in springtime.

These mid-winter celebrations existed long before the birthday of the Baby in Bethlehem pegged the calendar for the world and put its date-stamp on international coinage. Non-Christians as well as Christians can share the heritage of these festivities. Wassail and worship are legitimate companions at this season.

Because it is a winter festival for half the world it is naturally associated with hearth and home and is a time for families and friends to be together.

For many the image of Christmas is of glowing fires, steaming meals, Yule logs, and the carols and crafts of the winter fireside. Being a festival of long dark nights it is also in a sense a festival of light. The warm, flickering glow of candlelight and the timelessness of starlight symbolize perhaps the twin aspects of home and heaven. This treasury of Christmas has attempted to capture something of all these things. It has also explored the Christmas traditions of a wider world.

What of the hemisphere where Christmas falls nearer mid-summer than mid-winter? Reindeer and candlewax and frosted windows are a far cry from Papua New Guinea or the tropical palm beaches of Australia. But the heart of Christmas is the same the whole world over. The customs and the trappings may vary, but the 'magic' is the same. The candlelight may be local; the starlight is universal.

What is this magic, this extra dimension? The 'Love that comes down at Christmas' is an enricher and it is also a reconciler. Another more modern carol, but now a universal favourite, entitled 'The Cowboy Carol', speaks of 'a new world beginnin' from tonight'. Perhaps part of the magic of Christmas is the hope that the rebirth and renewal of nature can be reflected in families and in nations.

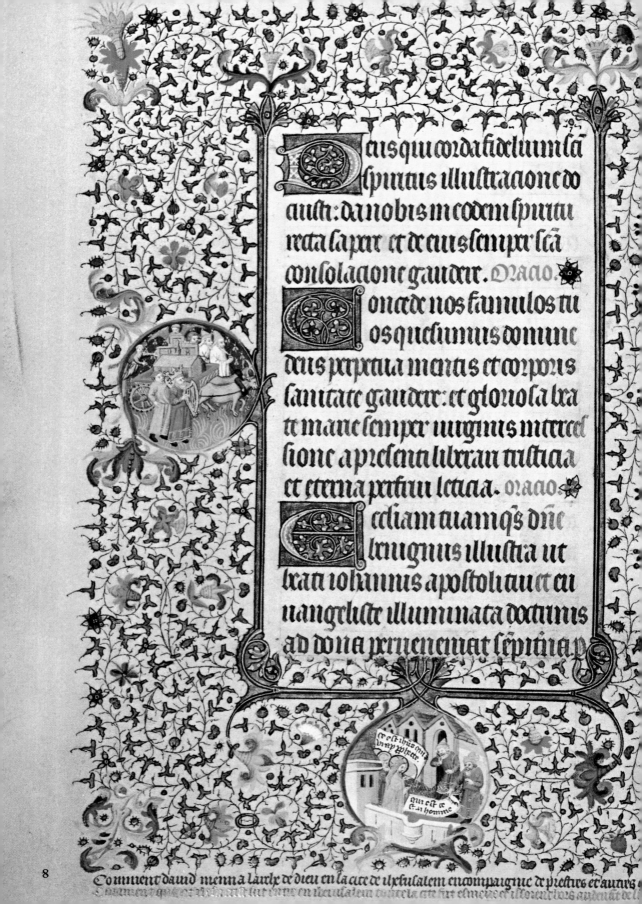

Deus qui corda fidelium sancti spiritus illustracione docuisti: da nobis in eodem spiritu recta sapere et de eius semper sancta consolacione gaudere. Oracio.

Concede nos famulos tuos quesumus domine deus perpetua mentis et corporis sanitate gaudere: et gloriosa beate marie semper uirginis intercessione a presenti liberari tristicia et eterna perfrui leticia. Oracio.

Ecclesiam tuam quesumus domine benignus illustra ut beati iohannis apostoli tui et euangeliste illuminata doctrinis ad dona perueniat sempiterna. p

Comment dauid mena larche de dieu en la cite de iherusalem encompaignie de prestres et autres

The First Christmas

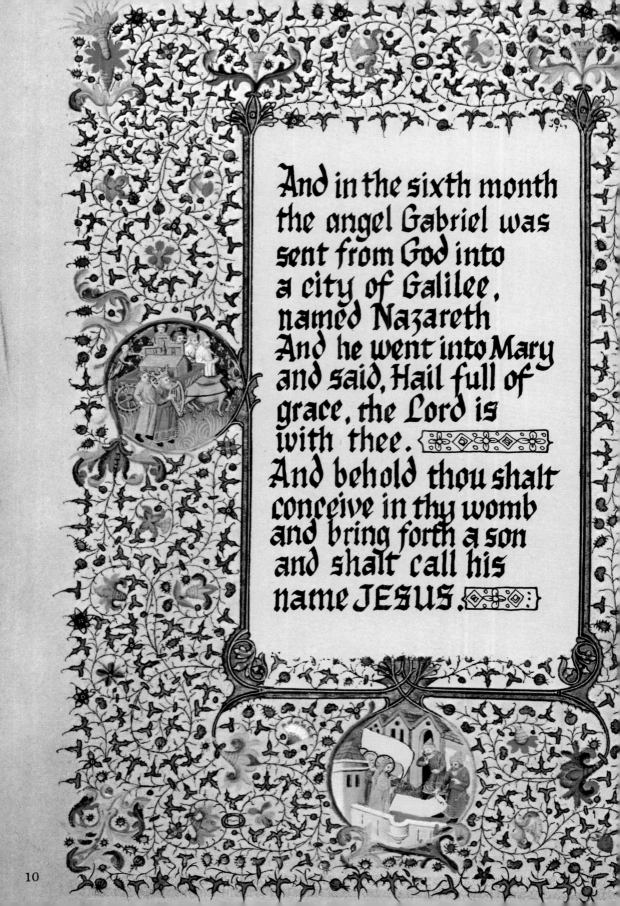

And in the sixth month the angel Gabriel was sent from God into a city of Galilee, named Nazareth And he went into Mary and said, Hail full of grace, the Lord is with thee. And behold thou shalt conceive in thy womb and bring forth a son and shalt call his name JESUS.

11

In laudibus.

eus in adiutoriu
meum intende.
Domine ad ad

Comme la benoite vierge marie ala visiter madame sainte helysabeth sa cousine laquelle lui dist q̃
de son ventre estoit benoit. Et estoit la dite helysabeth enseinte du benoit saint iehan baptist

And it came to pass that when Elisabeth heard the salutation of Mary, the babe leaped in her womb; and Elisabeth was filled with the Holy Spirit: And she spake out with a loud voice, and said, Blessed art thou among women, and blessed is the fruit of thy womb.

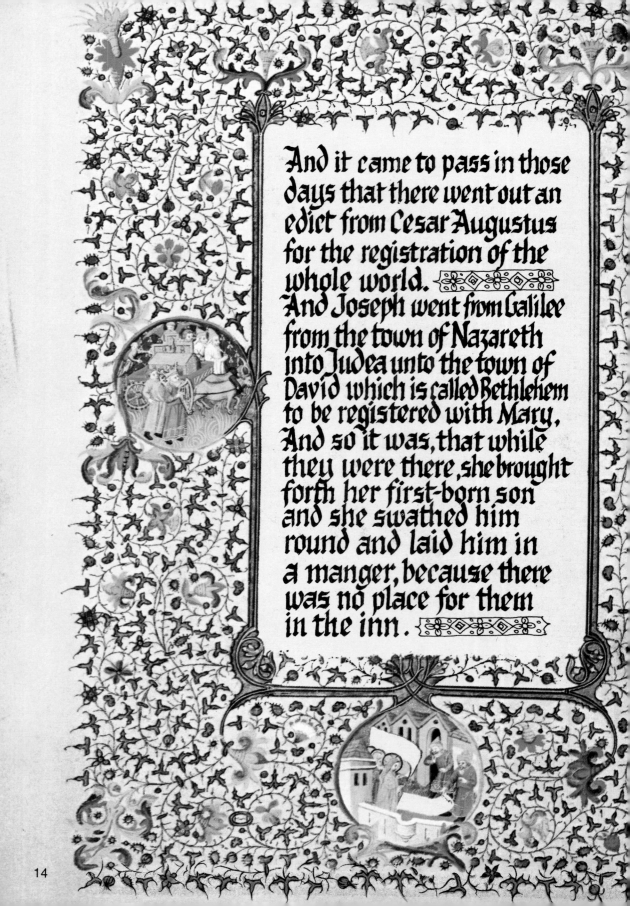

And it came to pass in those days that there went out an edict from Cesar Augustus for the registration of the whole world. And Joseph went from Galilee from the town of Nazareth into Judea unto the town of David which is called Bethlehem to be registered with Mary, And so it was, that while they were there, she brought forth her first-born son and she swathed him round and laid him in a manger, because there was no place for them in the inn.

Eus in Adprimam.
adiutorium meum
intende. ✦❉✦❉✦
Domine ad adiuuandum

Ens ad teriam.

ma dintorum
meum intende.

Dominie ad aduiuandum

Comment lange de paradis annonca aux pastoureaux la nativite de nostre seigneur ihesu crist
Comment les pastoureaux enfont grant ioye. et regardent contre mont come helbais menar st

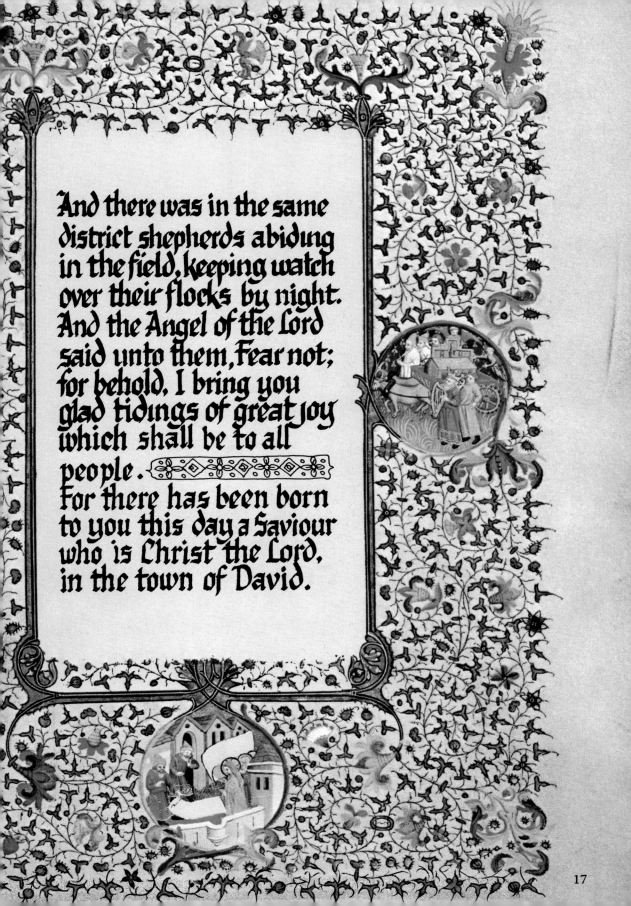

And there was in the same district shepherds abiding in the field, keeping watch over their flocks by night. And the Angel of the Lord said unto them, Fear not; for behold, I bring you glad tidings of great joy which shall be to all people.

For there has been born to you this day a Saviour who is Christ the Lord, in the town of David.

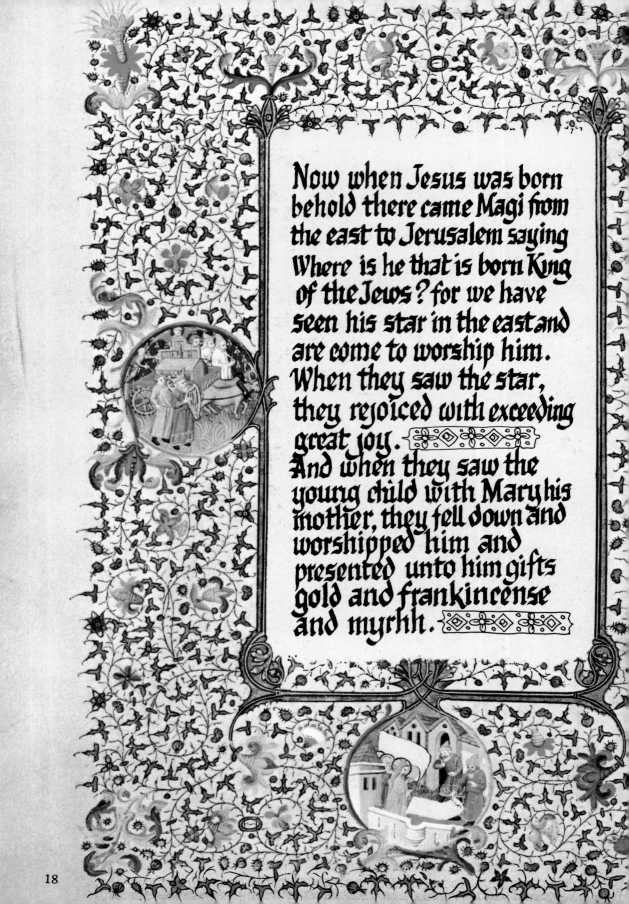

Now when Jesus was born behold there came Magi from the east to Jerusalem saying Where is he that is born King of the Jews? for we have seen his star in the east and are come to worship him. When they saw the star, they rejoiced with exceeding great joy.

And when they saw the young child with Mary his mother, they fell down and worshipped him and presented unto him gifts gold and frankincense and myrhh.

And when they were
departed, behold, the angel
of the Lord appeareth to
Joseph in a dream, saying
Arise, and take the young
child and his mother
and flee into Egypt, and
be thou there until I
bring thee word: For
Herod the king will seek
the young child to
destroy him.
When he arose, he took the
young child and his mother
by night and departed
into Egypt.

Deus in adiutorium
meum intende.
Domine ad ad
iuuandum me festina.

Christmas Around the World

St. Nicholas and Black Peter meeting children at Christmas in Holland.

From a rocky grotto
in Bethlehem celebrations
and customs have spread
for centuries across the
world. 'Light' conquering
darkness and 'Giving'
overcoming the spirit of
'Get' are two of their
themes.

Bethlehem in the snow.

A silver star marks the place where, Christians believe, the Son of God became Son of Man. Lamps, tended by different churches, burn perpetually above the sacred spot.

Each year, thousands of people from many lands come to Bethlehem in Israel to celebrate the birth of Jesus of Nazareth. Various churches hold services there on different dates: the Roman Catholics and Protestants on Christmas Eve, December 24; the Greek Orthodox, Syrians and Ethiopians on January 6; the Armenians on January 18. Other pilgrims and tourists visit the nearby Fields of the Shepherds, to whom the birth of the heavenly Child was said to have been announced by angels.

What happened in that 'Little Town of Bethlehem', the subject of many hymns since then, has affected people's lives and customs in every country. Only some of these customs can be given in this chapter. They range from Arctic Christmases where the temperature may be minus 25 degrees centigrade to India where it may be nearer 50 degrees centigrade (over 120 Fahrenheit).

Christmas customs go back to celebrations and rituals performed long before Christ's birth in Bethlehem. Teutonic and Celtic tribes held November feasts called *'Jiuleis'* or *'Giuli'*, from which the Scandinavian 'Jul' and our 'Yule' may come. Cattle were killed when the pasturage died off and the carcases roasted. The Yule log, symbol of fire, warmth and light to counter winter cold and darkness, was carefully prepared and lit. Its wood brought luck to the household.

In Roman times the Saturnalia was celebrated for a week from December 17, to mark a legendary Golden Age when Saturn ruled the world. Processions of men and women with garlands on their heads carrying lighted tapers took place and candles and green wreaths were given as presents. Distinctions of class and wealth were forgotten for that week and during the Kalends of January which followed. Slaves changed roles with their owners, rich and poor feasted as equals and took part in games and dances.

The Christian Church used to celebrate the birth of Christ on January 6, but in the 4th century found it convenient to take over the sacred pagan day of December 25, the winter solstice, which was chosen by the Emperor Aurelian in A.D. 274 as *Dies Natalis Invicti Solis,* Birthday of the Unconquered Sun. It was the chief festival of the Phrygian god Attis and of Mithras, whose worship was brought to Britain and other lands by the Roman army.

Pope Julius I, after careful enquiry into an earlier tradition that December 25 was the birthday of Jesus, made the date official. The birthday of the sun became the birthday of the Son of God. The gifts were in memory of the gifts brought to the Christ Child and to help people conquer selfishness and aid the poor. The lights were to symbolise the Light of the World. In England the celebration was called *'Christes masse',* the mass or church festival of Christ.

St. Boniface, who went from England to convert Germany in the 8th century, cut down a sacred oak at Geismar one Christmas Eve, and is said to have offered the outraged pagans a young fir tree instead, as a symbol of the new faith. The Christmas fir tree, established in Germany, became widely used in Britain early in Queen Victoria's reign. A large tree, sent each year from Norway to stand in London's Trafalgar Square, is a thank offering for Britain's help in World War II.

Eskimo children celebrating by eating kiviak—a great delicacy.

GREENLAND

In a village of Polar Eskimos near Thule in Greenland there is much visiting of families, drinking coffee and eating cakes and giving of brightly wrapped parcels, which may contain a model sledge, a pair of polished walrus tusks, or sealskin mitts. Everyone in the village gets a gift and children go from hut to hut, singing songs.

Christmas trees have to be imported, as no trees grow this far north. They are decorated, as in many lands, with candles and bright ornaments. Dancing goes on most of the night. After coffee, cakes and carols, a great delicacy called '*mattak*', whaleskin with a strip of blubber inside, is passed around. It tastes like fresh coconut, but is too tough to chew and is usually swallowed.

The Norwegian Christmas Nisse.

Another festive food is 'kiviak'. Although a delicacy to Eskimos it would not suit unaccustomed palates as it consists of the raw flesh of little auks which have been buried whole in sealskin for several months until they have reached an advanced stage of decomposition.

This is the one night in the year when the men look after the women, serving their coffee and stirring it for them. Games follow, including one in which an object is passed from hand to hand round a long table under the cloth. It is supposed to be repulsive: round, clammy and rough in texture, such as a frozen egg, wrapped in strips of wet fox fur!

NORWAY

A great baking of seven different kinds of biscuit is a feature of Norwegian preparations for Christmas. In fact, the sudden thaw which follows the year's first heavy snows before Christmas is called the 'biscuit thaw' because the heat of all the ovens is said to cause it!

Tall Christmas trees are decorated and wreaths to hang from the ceilings are made from cranberry bushes decorated with candles and ribbons. Christmas hymns and songs are sung around a tree, with actions to match the words. One such song is about the Nisse, a little gnome-like miniature Father Christmas, who expected his porridge outside the door but the family had forgotten to put it out, so all sorts of accidents happened to them and their cattle.

SWEDEN

In Sweden, Saint Lucia Day, December 13, opens the Christmas season.

Lucia was a Christian virgin martyred in 4th-century Syracuse, under the Emperor Diocletian. One legend says that she brought food each night to fellow Christians hiding underground in the catacombs. In order to have her hands free she carried lights in her hair.

Christianised Swedish Vikings heard of her story, and imagined her surrounded with a halo of light. Her festival is celebrated all over Sweden in both the towns and countryside, and even in offices and factories.

Very early in the morning, even at 3 or 4 a.m., a young daughter of each family puts on a long-sleeved white robe which reaches to the floor, with a red sash round the waist. In a wreath of greenery on her head, she places seven lighted candles. She serves the family in their beds with coffee, Lucia buns and *pepparkakor* or ginger snaps. Sons of the family escort her as 'Star Boys' in long white shirts with pointed paper hats. She sings the 'Santa Lucia' song to an old Italian melody.

A Stockholm newspaper in 1927 campaigned for processions in which Lucia, clad in white fur, led the way through the streets and incidentally stimulated Christmas buying. The current Nobel Prize winner in literature crowns an official Lucia, who spreads light and joy in a day of visits to hospitals, nursing homes and orphanages.

In the United States, Swedish-American organisations carry out Lucia celebrations with electrically-lit candles in Lucia's crown. These are for safety reasons, in line with the U.S. and Canadian custom of having electric lights on Christmas trees instead of 'live' candles.

Straw (*julhalm*) once played an important part in Yule ceremonies. It was thought to have magical properties and to bring luck to future harvests. Today, straw survives only in the straw stars that hang from Christmas-tree boughs or the crown of straw, called '*oro*' (unrest), that swings in ceaseless motion in the heat of the candles. A straw billy goat, once a sinister devil-figure, harmlessly guards the Christmas tree, while a sheaf of unthreshed grain is put out for the birds. Farmers think that large flocks of birds at Christmas improve prosperity for the coming year.

By Christmas Eve, Swedish housewives have to have their houses spotlessly clean. The farmer must have his tools indoors in their proper places or the wandering shoemaker from Jerusalem might pause to rest on them and bewitch them. In rural households each member has a *julhög* or pyramid of bread, cakes and fruit. Christmas Eve is often called Dipping Day from the custom of dipping rye bread in hot cooking liquid from Christmas ham.

On Christmas Day an early service called *Julotta* in candle-lit churches is very popular.

FINLAND

Christmas has become a secular holiday for many people in Finland, with the time before Christmas becoming very exhausting.

A Finnish artist recently drew a cartoon in one of the newspapers. It showed people rushing in and out of shops buying things, pushing each other, tired, quarrelling, loaded down with parcels of food and gifts, in a street sparkling with lights and decorations. Nobody noticed a little child standing in a dark corner wearing thin clothes, freezing and hungry, looking at all this going on. Under the picture was the caption: 'Birthday child watching the celebration of his birthday.'

But there are signs of a reaction, and people are going to Christmas services who used to go to churches only for weddings and funerals.

Christmas preparations start early in Finland and other Scandinavian countries with the First Sunday of Advent or 'Little Christmas'. There are three other Advent Sundays before Christmas. One candle is lit and put either in a special candlestick that holds four, or as the first of four candles on the Christmas tree. Children get their first Christmas present then. Small children get a calendar with a window to open each day before Christmas.

Usually all the family help to make gingerbread or 'pepparkakor'—in the shape of stars, hearts, moons, pigs and other figures, or gingerbread houses. The smell of gingerbread starts the real waiting for Christmas. The custom has been going since the 15th century.

Cold ham is the main food. In the days before refrigerators salted pork kept well. Salted meat and salted and pickled herrings are also eaten, as is herring salad with chopped carrots, turnips or salted cucumber, when fruit is expensive or difficult to get.

People take flowers—tulips, hyacinths or poinsettias—or gifts to friends. Then they gather at home round the decorated Christmas tree and drink a cup of *glogg*, made of red wine, spices and raisins.

The start of the main Christmas celebration is announced at twelve o'clock on December 24 by the Mayor of Helsinki. Everyone, he says, should pay their respects to the birth of Christ, so early on Christmas morning, about six o'clock, everyone gets up to go to church. The churches are lit with candles at all the pews, but sometimes the snow is too deep to get there in cars, so people have to watch a service on television.

HOLLAND

Saint Nicholas, the original saintly bishop and friend of children, is honoured for his true self in Holland. December 6 is his day and a great one for children, though Saint Nicholas parties are most commonly planned for Christmas Eve.

The saint arrives by steamer in Amsterdam harbour wearing a bishop's robe and mitre, white gloves and a large episcopal ring on his left hand. He is seated on a white horse and accompanied by Black Peter, who is partly a dark-skinned faithful servant and partly representing the devil in some respects, as a scourge of naughty children.

Thousands of children and adults cheer as Saint Nicholas in his scarlet mantle and Black Peter descend the gangplank. Church bells ring as the parade starts with a motorcade of police and a brass band in front. Saint Nicholas follows with Black Peter at his side. Then come the mayor and civic leaders. There are decorated floats, a cavalcade of students and more brass bands. The procession stops in the main square in front of the Royal Palace and Saint Nicholas is welcomed by the Queen.

Simple but subtly wrapped mystery presents are given at the Saint Nicholas parties. Hot punch or milk chocolate is drunk and dishes of boiled chestnuts eaten with butter and salt.

On December 26 there is a great outburst of singing and musical performances given by almost all Dutch music societies, radio groups and school choirs in church and concert halls and on radio and television, as if to greet the Saviour's coming.

IRELAND

The wren, the wren, the king of all birds On St. Stephen's day was caught in the furze

Christmas for the Irish lasts from Christmas Eve to the feast of Epiphany on January 6, which Irish people call 'Little Christmas'. After sunset on Christmas Eve, the father of the house puts a tall, thick candle on the sill of the largest window. The youngest member of the family, in honour of the infant Jesus, is usually chosen to light the candle. It is left to burn all night to any, who, like Mary and Joseph, may be looking for shelter. Sometimes many candles are put in the windows, and in Ireland any wanderers are given hospitality and sent on their way with a gift of money at this season. The women will be baking a round cake, full of caraway seeds, for each person in the house.

The day after Christmas Day, St. Stephen's Day, is almost as important as Christmas Day for the Irish. In Ireland itself, football and horseracing are popular sports for adults. For children the Wren Boys Procession is the big event.

Young men and boys (sometimes girls also) are up early, dressed in gay clothes in some regions, in old clothes with faces blackened in other counties. In some southern districts they have home-made hoods over their heads with eyes cut out or masks of Mickey Mouse and Donald Duck. They march and sing to an accompaniment of violins, accordions, harmonicas and horns. They carry a long pole with a holly bush tied to its top.

This is supposed to contain a captured wren, and in less humane days a wren was actually killed and carried round in procession. Later, the wren took the tour in a stable lantern or, as in Wales, in a special 'wren house'. Sometimes called 'Feeding the Wren', the ceremony was used by young people to ask for money 'for the starving wren', i.e. their own empty pockets!

A rhyme for the occasion was:

'The wren, the wren, the king of all birds
On St. Stephen's day was caught in the furze.'

Above and below:
The Wren Boys.

All through the year the tiny wren, full-volumed in its song, is 'king of all birds'. This title was claimed, it is said, by a crafty wren who rode on an eagle's head and boasted he had 'flown higher than an eagle'. But for all his boasts he suffered a vendetta for many years at Christmas in Cornwall and Oxfordshire in England, and in the Isle of Man and France as well as in Ireland.

An Irish explanation for their former custom is a story that during a rebellion against English rule in the North a group of English soldiers were being surrounded as they slept. But wrens pecked on their drums and woke them, so the enemy soldiers escaped. The wren was called 'the Devil's bird' in Ireland. Wren-killing may in fact go back to the druids' use of wren song for divining the future, or to magic properties a wren's feathers were believed to possess.

SCOTLAND

Scots go to church on Christmas Eve and Day, but concentrate their main celebration on New Year's Eve or Hogmanay and New Year's day. They seem to have taken the Protestant reformers' attacks on the misuse of Christmas more seriously than the English did. That does not prevent a vast amount of drinking, the main feature of Hogmanay.

The word 'Hogmanay', according to one theory, may derive from an old French New Year custom called '*hoguinana*'. Those supporting this view refer to the 'Auld Alliance' between Scotland and France in the later Middle Ages and Tudor times.

Others believe the word comes from the cheese and oat cakes given to children on New Year's Eve, when they went in procession through the streets, covered in a long sheet like a Chinese dragon in a festival.

They recited a rhyme:

> *Get up, goodwife, and shake your feathers,*
> *And dinna think that we are beggars;*
> *For we are bairns come out to play,*
> *Get up and gie's our hogmanay.*

'First footing' is an important part of New Year's Day in Scotland and wherever Scots are in the world, and also in some northern counties of Britain. The first person to set foot in the house after midnight strikes and the Old Year ends, brings good or bad luck to the home. Any woman brings bad luck, so do flat-footed, lame or squint-eyed people. The First Foot man must, if possible, be a stranger with dark hair (in some districts he must be fair-haired). If strangers are not available, a friend can 'first foot', or one of the family may go out and come back with the traditional gifts of a piece of coal and bread, some money or salt.

These magic gifts are meant to ensure warmth, food and wealth to the family throughout the year. Sometimes the First Foot carries a branch of evergreen as a symbol of continuing life. A dark-haired man with all the other proper qualifications may arrange to 'first-foot' a whole group of houses. He will expect some whisky as a reward at each stop!

ENGLAND AND WALES

Christmas came to England when St. Augustine landed in Kent in A.D. 596 with 40 monks to bring Christianity to the Anglo-Saxons. On Christmas Day, a few years later, more than 10,000 English converts to the Christian faith were baptised. A century later, by the time of the historian Bede (who died in A.D. 734), Christmas was one of the three main festivals of the year, along with Epiphany and Easter.

Bede records that 'the ancient people of the Angli began their year on December 25th, when we celebrate the birthday of the Lord'. This result was a triumph for the diplomatic advice given by Pope Gregory when he sent Augustine and his team on their mission. They were not to destroy the well-built pagan temples, only the idols in them. 'Build altars and place relics in them . . . when this people see that their shrines are not destroyed, they will be able to banish error from their hearts and be more ready to come to the places they are familiar with, but now recognising and worshipping the true God.'

Opposite: *Old English music sheet.*

THE CHRISTMAS WAITS

J. BRANDARD.

M & N. HANHART

COMIC QUADRILLE BY
HENRI LAURENT.

The Church and the robust island peoples, who mostly worked on the land, rubbed shoulders. No doubt more rubbed off the clerical shoulders on to their flocks than the other way round. But there was always a two-way traffic, as the lower orders of clergy were drawn from peasant stock.

At the turn of the first 1,000 years after Christ, Ethelred with his laws and Edward the Confessor with his decrees had established that Christmas was to be a time of peace and concord. That could appeal to those with secular or spiritual outlooks and church men and women constantly strove to make the spiritual current the stronger one in the tides of their age.

Holly, for instance, one of the evergreen decorations used in homes and churches, was believed by village folk to keep witches and tax-collectors away. Christians made wreaths of it as symbols of Christ's crown of thorns, placed on His head by Roman soldiers before they led Him out to his crucifixion. The red berries were said to represent drops of His blood. Ivy, on the other hand, remained pagan, being linked with wreaths round the reeling brow of the Roman wine god Bacchus.

Songs at Yuletide pointed to holly as the male and ivy as the female. In an anecdote, an English knight is said to have invited his tenants and their wives to Christmas dinner. "But before you eat, Holly," he said with a mischievous look at the men, "any one of you who is master of his wife must sing a carol." Only one fellow got up and nervously sang a carol.

The knight then turned to the women's table and said, "Ivy, it's your turn. Whoever is master of her husband is to sing a carol as proof." At which, says the tale, 'they fell all to such singing that there never was heard such a caterwauling piece of music'. The knight laughed and declared: "The ivy is the master."

Trees play a part to this day in the folklore and customs of England's Christmas. The Glastonbury Thorn is said to owe its origin to Joseph of Arimathea, who arranged for Christ's body to be buried after the Crucifixion. Soon after, he is said to have landed in Britain to spread the Faith. Tired of his journey from the Isle of Avalon, he stuck his thorn staff in the ground and went to sleep on what is now called Weary-All Hill. When he woke, he found it had taken root and was to flower at Christmas time. Every year thousands come to see it flower either at Christmas 'new style' on December 25, or by the old calendar on January 6.

A Puritan in Elizabeth I's reign chopped down the tree as idolatrous, but pilgrims had taken and planted cuttings, so the tree's direct descendants survived. Each year, the Mayor of Glastonbury in Somerset and the local vicar cut sprays from the Thorn to send to Queen Elizabeth II for the Royal table on Christmas Day.

Sceptical modern botanists know the Thorn by its Latin

name, *Crataegus monogyna biflora*, which flowers twice a year. One of its flowerings is usually in the Christmas season.

Another plant is responsible for a Christmas custom only adopted in Britain. Mistletoe probably gets its name from *misteltan*, meaning 'different twig', since it is a semi-parasite whose light green dense growth contrasts with the host tree on which it grows. Celtic Druids regarded it as sacred. They cut and used it with elaborate rituals and as a result it was banned in churches, but it came in handy in homes, where its use probably reflected an early fertility or marriage rite.

Girls who stand under a sprig or bunch of mistletoe hanging in a house are fair game for kissing. The custom never seems to have been taken up in other countries—possibly because Mediterranean men, at least, need no mistletoe to urge them on! But it may also have come about in England for the opposite reason, namely that in Tudor and early Stuart times the English were much given to kissing. Erasmus wrote in the 16th century that in England 'wherever you go everyone welcomes you with a kiss and the same on bidding farewell'. The custom seems to have been gaining ground again in recent years.

The Glastonbury Thorn.

Many local customs in counties and villages are special to England and Wales. A variant of the Yule log is the Devon burning of the ashen faggot. The ash tree has always been linked to witchcraft, and divination was practised while it burned. In a more harmless use, the faggot was tied with nine bands of green ash. Each unmarried girl in the household would choose a band. She whose band burst first would be first to marry. In the Luttrell Arms Hotel, Dunster, in Somerset, the ash faggot is still lit on Christmas Eve and a round of hot punch is drunk each time a band bursts.

In Wales, mummers continue the ancient custom of *Mari Lwyd* (Grey Mare) at Pencoed near Maesteg and Llangynwyd in Glamorgan. The word 'mummer' seems to derive from Greek and German words meaning 'a mask' or 'masker'. *Mari Lwyd* was the name given to the horse turned out of its stable to make room for Jesus and His family. The horse has been looking, it is said, for shelter ever since.

At *Mari Lwyd* the chief mummer wears a skeleton horse's head, decorated with ribbons and bottle-glass eyes. The man is hidden under a white cloth, once probably a shroud or animal skin, with the head on a long pole. He can open and shut the horse's jaws and the 'horse' chases and bites anyone it can catch, only releasing them when they pay a forfeit.

With the horse are stock characters of a mummers' play: Leader, Merryman, Punch and Judy and Sergeant. Recalling past feuds, householders at first refuse to let the mummers in, but finally they are let in and entertained.

The Devil's Knell has been tolled at Dewsbury in Yorkshire on Christmas Eve for over 700 years. The bell, rung once for every year since Christ's birth, is supposed to mark the Devil's departure from Earth—and especially from Dewsbury. The bell is called Black Tom of Soothill and is named after Thomas de Soothill, a 13th-century gentleman who is said to have killed one of his servants. As a penance he presented the bell to the church.

Mystery or miracle plays, which are performed to this day in York and Chester, were a more elaborate custom and a contrast to the pagan mummers, giving the story of the birth of Christ with shepherds, first roistering, then reverent.

FRANCE

Crèche is a French word for manger or crib, and one little French town has become world-famous for its little figures used in Christmas cribs. It is Aubagne, a modest little Provençal town about halfway between Marseilles and Aix-en-Provence, and is, somewhat incongruously perhaps, the home of the French Foreign Legion.

Though St. Francis of Assisi introduced crèches in 1224, making them only became widespread in the 16th century. In France most churches used large cribs before the Revolution of 1789, but only in the 19th century did they come to be widely used in French homes.

In Aubagne, craftsmen make unbaked clay figures called *santons* or 'little saints'. A Marseilles man, Jean Louis Lagnel, who survived the anti-clerical persecutions of the Revolution, started to produce *santons* for a world market and held his first *Foire aux Santons*, a 'little saints' festival', in 1803. He included Provençal characters along with the traditional Jesus, Mary, Joseph, kings, shepherds and animals. With the shepherds in Provençal dress you may find a poacher—honoured for enterprise, no doubt—a gendarme, a miller, fishwife, woman musician, village simpleton (*le ravi*). A parish priest recently added enlarged snapshots of local celebrities, blending in with the background.

French children put out shoes or *sabots*, wooden clogs, in the hearth for the Christ Child or Father Christmas (Père Noel) to fill. Adults give each other presents at New Year. When Christmas Eve festivities are over and the family has gone to bed it is the custom to leave a fire burning, candles lit and food and drink on the table, in case the Virgin Mary passes that way.

Three masses are held during the night in beautifully lit churches and cathedrals, from whose bells and carillons Christmas carols ring out. Then the family returns home to a meal known as le réveillon. It may be of roast fowl, baked ham, salads, cake, fruit and wine. But in Alsace a goose has pride of place. In Brittany there are buckwheat cakes and sour cream. Burgundians eat turkey and chestnuts. In the Paris region oysters are the favourite dish, followed by a cake shaped like a Yule log.

GERMANY

Christmas trees twinkle and blaze with light in the squares of German towns and cities on Christmas Eve. For it was Germany that gave the world the custom of lighting and decorating small fir trees. St. Boniface, English apostle to the Germans, is credited with starting the custom.

Another story says Martin Luther began the custom in the 16th century. He used the candle-lit tree to symbolise the starry heavens from which Christ came. A writer in Strasbourg in 1605 says that citizens there put little fir trees in their parlours and decorated them with paper roses, apples and sweets.

Because Luther was linked with the custom, it mainly spread over Protestant parts of Europe. America adopted it before it came to England. Hessian soldiers from Germany in George III's army are said to have set up Christmas trees in the snowy campaigns against George Washington's men. German and German-Swiss settlers in Pennsylvania also had their trees.

Advent wreaths, with a candle to be lit on each of the four Sundays leading up to Christmas, are accompanied by cakes and coffee on those mornings. They mark the days to Holy Evening, the most sacred time of the German Christmas. Though the traveller may see the Christmas trees twinkling outside, most Germans will be indoors with family and friends. On the doors hang wreaths of evergreen. The song 'O Tannenbaum' about the fir tree shows that Germans regard it as a symbol of loyalty and evergreen and fresh life, even in the darkest days.

But not everyone is indoors yet. In Berchtesgaden in Bavaria young men form up in long lines on the mountains and fire pistols or special mortars. Today this is done to honour Christ's birth and the elevation of the Sacrament at Midnight Mass, but originally, like Somerset farmers firing guns through apple trees, it was to awaken sleeping vegetation and drive away evil spirits.

In this region also, St. Nicholas visits homes in the first week of Advent, attended by a boy dressed as a girl called 'Nikolo-Weibl' or 'little Nicholas woman'. With him are 12 Buttenmandeln, young men dressed in straw with animal masks over their heads. Cowbells tied on their bodies make a terrific clanging noise. The Bishop gives a short sermon, Nikolo-Weibl hands out gifts, the Buttenmandeln fall on the young people present and drive them out of the house with shouts and blows. This rough treatment was in origin probably a pagan cult to ensure good fortune and crops. It is now explained as a punishment for idleness and bad conduct.

Children receive their presents primarily from the Christkind or Christ Child, who may be represented as a white-robed figure wearing a golden crown and having big golden wings.

On Christmas Eve in some parts of Germany a table is set between the family Christmas tree and an open window, on which is a soup plate for each child. Next day the Christ Child is credited with filling the plates with sweets and fruit. More valuable presents are found on the table. In Westphalia children write letters for the Christ Child to read.

In addition to visits by the Christkind (sometimes corrupted into Kriss Kringle) Saint Nicholas goes about checking children's behaviour and sometimes displaying embarrassingly intimate knowledge of their sins. For naughty ones he leaves bundles of rods as a warning, while good ones get little presents. Knecht (knight) Rupprecht may take his place at times. Both of them can read people's minds and know their secret thoughts and deeds.

Rupprecht, sometimes called ru-Klas or Rough Nicholas in robust northern lands, is dressed in skins or straw and may be an older pagan spirit. Today in north Germany he examines children in their Christian prayers and punishes them if they fail his tests.

Corn features in south Germany as in many other countries. It is strewn on housetops to include the birds in the feast. In Silesia, now in East Germany, where Christmas is discouraged, peasants sometimes carry wheat to church on Christmas Day and afterwards give it to the poultry as a safeguard against poultry diseases and to promote growth and egg laying.

ITALY

In Italy the Christmas season starts eight days before Christmas and goes on till after Twelfth Night or the Feast of Epiphany. On December 23, or earlier, children dressed as shepherds with sandals, leggings tied with crossing thongs, and wearing shepherds' hats, go from house to house playing songs on shepherds' pipes and giving recitations. They are given coins to buy Christmas delicacies. In cities like Rome some real shepherds sometimes carry out this performance.

Families centre their Christmas round a *presepio*, the manger or crib, representing in miniature the Holy Family in the stable. Guests kneel in front of it and musicians sing before it. No meat is eaten for 24 hours before Christmas Eve, but there follows a meal as big as the family can afford.

In Rome cannon boom out from the Castle of St. Angelo to proclaim the opening of the Holy Season. Each church tries to exhibit the biggest or most artistic *presepio*. *Ara Coeli,* the Altar of Heaven, is considered one of the most beautiful with its golden figure of the baby Jesus. People write to Him from all over the world, asking for help and miracles. There are great stacks of cards and envelopes to be seen round the crib at Christmas. Silver hearts are brought by those who have experienced miracles.

January 6 marks the day the Magi came. Gifts are brought by a benevolent witch called *Befana,* a corruption of Epiphania. She comes down the chimney and fills the good children's shoes with presents, but leaves only pieces of charcoal for the bad ones.

A special New Year Banquet is eaten on the last day of the year, with raisin bread, turkey, chicken, rabbit and spaghetti. Champagne corks pop at midnight.

SICILY

Sicilians fast from sunset on December 23 to sunset on December 24. Then a great Yule log is kindled. After prayers and songs round the *presepio* (the crib, as in Italy) the feast begins. There may be eels and larks, boiled pasta, fish, sweet bread and *torrone* (nougat).

At midnight church services are packed with worshippers. As in Naples and some other Italian towns, men and boys come down from the mountains dressed as shepherds and play their Sicilian bagpipes called *ciamarelle.* In Italy the pipers are called *zampognari.*

And as in Italy, children await the visit of *La Befana* on January 6. This good woman befriended the Three Wise Men, but was so busy cleaning her house, it is said, that she missed going with them to Bethlehem. She is probably a survival of a pagan character, for she is a sort of benevolent witch, with cane in one hand for naughty children and bell in the other to announce her arrival. Children hang their stockings up for her, and she fills them with toys and gifts.

PORTUGAL

In Portugal, families eat the *consoada* or Christmas banquet in the early hours of Christmas Day. The *fogueira da consoada* or Yule log burns at the hearth or sometimes in the churchyards. The family preserve the ashes and charred remains of the log and pinecones burnt in the fire and later, in the thunderstorm season of the year, they burn these remains. Where the smoke goes, they believe, no thunderbolt will strike.

Old magic customs still hang on. The souls of the dead, the *alminhas a penar,* are abroad at Christmas, but families welcome rather than fear them. Crumbs are scattered for them on the hearth.

Dragging in the Yule log.

This is a hangover from the custom of entrusting seeds to the dead so that they can bring them back as fruits or grain at harvest.

The table is left spread after the *consoada* so that departed loved ones can share its plenty. Their souls might be seen as little flickering lights. In Minho province they only come if no prayers are offered for their peace.

GREECE

Christmas is widely celebrated in Greece, though Easter is the main holiday, as in other lands of the Eastern Orthodox Church. Boys sing carols to the accompaniment of drum beating and tinkling steel triangles before Christmas Eve Mass. They are rewarded with dried figs, walnuts, almonds and sweets in the villages and with money in the towns.

Mass starts at 4 a.m. and ends before daybreak. There follows a family meal featuring *Christpsomo*, 'bread of Christ', a cake decorated with nuts and *kourabiedes*, small cakes covered with powdered sugar or soaked in honey.

Greeks do not use Christmas trees or give presents at Christmas. A priest may throw a little cross into the village water to drive the *kallikantzari* (gremlin-like spirits) back to their haunts. To keep them from hiding in forgotten corners he goes from house to house sprinkling holy water.

U.S.S.R.

In the Soviet Union the religious festival of Christmas is being replaced by the Festival of Winter, the component elements of which are New Year's carols with a new non-religious content. Official policy is to replace 'Father Christmas' with 'Grandfather Frost'. An article in *Izvestia* of December 26, 1974, reports celebrations on Pushkin Square in Moscow with 'Grandfather Frost' and 25 'forest beauties' in the form of trees, animals and folklore characters. Folk-songs round the tree and old Russian games were organised.

A report in *Pravda* of December 30, 1973, tells of similar festivities including the Snow Maiden and a New Year tree for 75,000 schoolchildren. Pictures show a large tree in the Hall of Columns in the Kremlin with several hundred children holding hands round it. 'Grandfather Frost', with round white fur hat, beard and red coat trimmed with broad bands of fur, and with staff in hand, is leading a procession.

But celebrations of Christmas with its original truths go on. An article in the *Baptist Times* of January 1, 1976, reports services being held, using January 7 and 8 as Christmas Eve and Day respectively. Christmas hymns with the theme of the Incarnation are sung. 'These services,' says the paper's correspondent, 'are regarded as a great Evangelical opportunity. Great crowds gather to share in the worship. Many of the churches are decorated with Christmas trees, flowers and coloured lights.'

Grandfather Frost.

Besides the services in church, family worship has a special place in the Christmas celebrations of believers who invite friends to their homes to share in simple, homely celebration. There are, of course, special meals as well, although Russian people do not associate any particular food with Christmas, like turkey, duck or Christmas pudding. The exchange of cards and presents takes place only on a modest scale. The commercialisation of Christmas has not reached the Soviet Union, but gifts are presented and received and greetings are exchanged, especially among believers.

An old print of a children's Christmas procession in Russia.

No doubt some Christmas customs of old days persist in the Ukraine, where a 39-day fast used to precede the Nativity. Young and old would wait till they saw the first star in the sky. 'The star, Mother, I see the star,' they would cry. This was the signal for the 12-course supper to begin, one course in honour of each of the 12 apostles. Fish took the place of meat. There would be *borsch* (beet soup), cabbage stuffed with millet, and cooked dried fruit. The special Christmas Eve delicacy *kutya*, whole-wheat grains soaked for hours, seasoned with honey and crushed poppy seeds, would be served. Hay was spread on floor and table to encourage horse-feed for the coming year, and humans clucked to encourage hens to lay eggs!

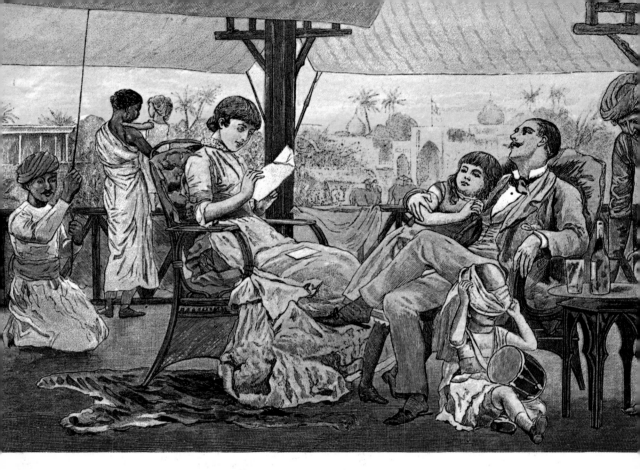

A 19th-century print of a British family celebrating Christmas in India.

PAKISTAN

In Pakistan, December 25 is a public holiday, but it is in memory of Jinnah, the founder of Pakistan. In Christian households cards and gifts are exchanged, new clothes are worn and friends' houses visited.

From the Christian villages people pack services on Christmas Day, which in Urdu and Punjabi is called *Bara Din,* the Big Day. Punjabis like bright clothes so it is a gay occasion. People embrace in Punjabi style with the greeting *'Bara Din Mubarrak Ho',* 'the blessing of Christmas on you'.

BANGLADESH

In Bangladesh, formerly East Pakistan, Christian village men cut down scores of banana trees and replant them in pairs along the paths to churches and outside their homes. They bend over the huge leaves to make an arch, and then make small holes in the bamboo poles, fill them with oil and tie them across the arches. When the oil is lit, the way to church is bright.

Right and below: *Indian paintings of the Madonna and Child, and the visit of the Magi.*

INDIA

Christians in India are a minority, and their celebrations are a mixture of Eastern and Western traditions. Indians have their own Hindu Festival of Light, *Diwali*, symbolising the conquest of darkness by light a few months earlier. This helps them to understand the Christian festival.

In the villages Indian Christians send trays of fruits, nuts, sweets and flowers to friends and relatives. But in the towns the Western custom of exchanging cards has largely taken this over. There are new clothes for the family, gifts and Indian festal dishes. In most churches there are cribs and tableaux showing the Christ Child with Mary and Joseph.

In many parts of India, shops are made attractive with lights, ribbons and simulated snowflakes. Recorded Christmas carols put shoppers in a mood to buy. Christmas-card sellers do a brisk trade. The pictures on the cards give an Indian setting to the Christmas story, which may be nearer to the original Middle Eastern surroundings of simplicity and poverty.

Indian Christians do not believe in short services, a quick address and then home, but go in for mammoth services. Time is no object. The main service on Christmas Day is a midnight service which lasts from two and a half to three hours, with hundreds of communicants and many children all massed together on the floor. Candles and floral arrays of scarlet poinsettias are everywhere. Outside, decorations are often done with whole banana trees, making India one of the few places in the world where poinsettias can be seen growing on the banana trees!

In north-west India the tribal Christians of the Bhil folk, an aboriginal people, go out night after night for a week at Christmas to sing their equivalent of carols the whole night through. They go to surrounding villages where there are Christians or enquirers.

In south India Christians fill little clay lamps with oil and put a piece of twisted cotton into each for a wick. Towards the evening they light these lamps and place them along the edge of the low flat-roofed houses and along the walls outside, so that the houses twinkle with light. People who do not know that Christmas is the birthday of Jesus often ask: "Why do you have these lights in your houses now?" Then the Christian families tell them the Christmas story.

Their host spreads hay on the cow-dung floor of a mud-walled verandah to keep his visitors warm in the winter night, which can be cold in north-west India. A drum and cymbals accompany the song which may be set to a hot tribal rhythm. If there are many houses to be visited, they may not sing more than five or six tunes in one house, but as each hymn has 30 to 40 verses it doesn't take many visits before cocks crow at 4 a.m. or the sun rises at six! The host, however poor, will try to bring out a *thali* or tray filled with chunks of sweetmeat for the 40 or 50 people crowded on his verandah. On the fringe of the crowd will be non-Christian neighbours, attracted by the music, to listen to the message of Mary and her Baby.

Opposite: *Chinese painting illustrating the Flight into Egypt.*

HONG KONG

In Hong Kong Chinese Christians of many denominations celebrate Christmas with hundreds of church services in Chinese. At the Anglican Cathedral, services mainly attended by Europeans are in English, but about a fifth of the large congregation may be Chinese.

The Chinese traditionally concentrate on their New Year and save the main festivity till then. In Hong Kong and Taiwan, Chinese Christians send Christmas cards, many of which are exquisite examples of the art of a gifted people. In these the Holy Family have Chinese features and are in a Chinese setting. Poinsettias and Nativity scenes decorate homes, churches and public places, and big red and gold ideographs from their picture alphabet decorate streamers and paper chains. Santa Claus, who is known as *Lan Khoong* (Nice Old Father) or as *Dun Che Lao Ren* (Christmas Old Man) with his reindeer, are a surprising addition to the Far Eastern scene.

Left: *Christmas card in the Chinese by 'Poo Tung Pete'.*
Right: *Japanese painting of Nativity.*

JAPAN

Farther East in Japan there are only half a million Christians in a population of 110,000,000. Japanese have taken over Christmas largely as a commercial occasion with an American flavour. Christmas songs, mostly 'Jingle Bells' and 'Silent Night', blare out over loudspeakers. Shops advertise Christmas with decorations and encourage buying of gifts and Christmas cards. Many families have a Christmas cake, a richly iced and decorated sponge cake.

Christians use the chance to tell non-Christian friends the story of Jesus Christ, and radio and television carry the message to millions. One Sunday School collected money all the year to buy flowers to thank the police at the local police station for helping them in many ways. They bought a big cake and invited the police to a party. The police in turn brought sweets, did conjuring tricks and came with their brass band. The Sunday School told the police what Christianity meant.

A Japanese student told of the effect of Christmas on her at Kobe College: 'Before last Christmas I experienced Christmas only as enjoying myself and I held parties with my friends and feasted. Now I take a delight in serving others. At first I knitted socks for orphans and helped with the Christmas programme of the Sunday School. I had experienced the true Christmas spirit and am looking forward to such a Christmas again this year.'

Children at a Christmas party in Belize.

Folk carving of Madonna and Child.

NEW GUINEA

One pagan custom was changed through the Christmas story to create lasting peace between head hunting, cannibal tribes in New Guinea.

For the Sawi tribes of West Irian, treachery was an ideal and a way of life. The only sure way to peace was for a chief on each side to exchange an infant son as a 'peace child'. Each tribe looked after the adopted child most carefully, for if the child died the peace treaty would end and fighting would break out again.

Don Richardson, a young Canadian missionary, and his wife Carol told the Sawi that God had sent His only son to be a 'peace child' who could never die. After overcoming fear of their demons' reactions, many Sawis became Christians, gave up their treacheries and spread the new idea of a permanent peace child among their people.

In a book *Peace Child* Don tells of a Christmas morning when he and Carol with their two young sons were able to hold a large service-cum-feast to which Sawis invited enemy tribesmen to come in their canoes. The Sawis laid food gifts at their former enemies' feet and sang carols. A Sawi preacher read a verse from Isaiah: 'Unto us a child is born, to us a son is given.' The visitors could see in the transformed Sawi faces that the old ideals of treachery had indeed gone for good, conquered by the Babe of Bethlehem.

AUSTRALIA

The Australian Christmas Bush which flowers at Christmas.

Christmas is in the high summer in Australia, with temperatures as high as 110°F in the shade, which seems a long way from the cold winter's nights of the European Christmas.

Generally Christmas is celebrated along traditional lines and families often travel great distances to be together. Sometimes, however, they gather, not in their homes in the city or in the outback, but at a cottage by the sea, for Christmas is in the main summer holiday period. The holiday centres are packed, the roads to the beaches are jammed, yet the churches are filled for the Christmas Day services, often from very early in the morning. Many of the carols sung are Australian, celebrating Christ's birth with an imagery drawn from the bush.

There is not, of course, the contrast between the light and warmth of a European Christmas and the dark and cold of the nights outside. Nor is Christmas, as in Britain, a short and therefore contrasting break in a nation's work schedule, but a part of a long holiday period. Yet there is the same intensity of feeling about Christmas, and it is the most important event each year.

NEW ZEALAND

In New Zealand, Christmas is combined with summer holidays. So, as well as present-buying and parties, many families prepare to go off to the beaches. The shops are decorated with scenes familiar to countries like England—Father Christmas with his red cloak and white beard, snow scenes; all this means Christmas to many whose parents or grandparents came out from Europe.

Here, as in many countries, everyone can be so busy celebrating that they may forget *what* they are celebrating.

John, a solicitor in Auckland, and his wife Mary felt somehow they would like the message of Christmas to mean something to their two children, and the children of their friends. Auckland is a large city in the North Island, and many Pacific islands are all around. Many islanders make their home there and many races mingle, yet have their separate traditions. Richard and Mary felt they'd like the children to understand that the Christmas festival was something for the whole world. They began to think of families they knew who might like to come to a special party. They were loaned a hall in a Catholic hospital, invited their friends and their friends invited others. Everyone, it seemed, accepted—however busy they were. This was to be a different kind of Christmas party, not the giving of expensive presents, or a party where a lot of money was spent on Christmas lights and decorations, but something real and simple, in the spirit of the first Christmas, when Jesus Christ was born.

The evening of the party arrived. The hall was decorated with large vases of red pohutakawa blossoms, the New Zealand Christmas tree. There was also a tall pine tree with lots of candles. All sat around, the children in front. The nursing sisters came in and sat quietly at the back.

A girl from Papua New Guinea had made a grass hut and inside was the crib she had made from bamboo. She spoke simply of what Christmas meant in her country. A woman from Tonga said they celebrate the whole night before Christmas Day. They go to church, sing carols, go round to their relatives and friends. It is a very happy time and a time of great rejoicing. A Swedish girl dressed in white, with candles all alight round her head, led a procession of other girls, also in white with candle headdresses.

Soon the lighting of the candles on the tree began. Each child took a light on the end of a stick and lit a candle for each country represented at the party. Some candles were too high up for the children so taller people had to help out! All the decorations on the tree were of natural materials, some of straw, such as they have in Scandinavian countries, then there were nuts, shining red apples and gingerbread figures. Young people from several countries, Malaya, Taiwan, Japan, North America, sang gaily. Everyone joined in the carols.

The story of the birth of Jesus seemed very appropriate as the teller emphasized that in Palestine in those days there were no motels—a common feature of New Zealand life—and how the shepherds on a sheep station saw a star. . . . Everyone grew silent. and in the silence the true meaning of Christmas came alive.

U.S.A.

Christmas in the United States has a wide variety of customs which the citizens of America brought from their lands of origin. This marriage of many ethnic traditions adds great richness to the American Christmas. Central to them all remain the exchange of gifts and greetings and family visits, while for many the day begins at Midnight Mass on Christmas Eve.

In the South the custom has been to celebrate noisily with fireworks and the shooting of firearms. Early settlers sent Christmas greetings in this way to distant neighbours. The practice may originally have been meant to frighten off evil spirits. It spread to Hawaii and the Philippines.

In Alaska 'going round with the star' is a feature of the season. Boys and girls with lanterns on poles carry a large figure of a star, covered with bright-coloured paper, from door to door. They sing carols and are welcomed in for refreshments. On the next night another party of boys and girls, dressed as Herod's men, try to destroy the infant Jesus.

Stars also feature in other parts of the United States. At Palmers Lake, Colorado, a star 500 feet in diameter on Sundance Peak can be seen for 20 miles around by travellers in cars and trains. On South Mountain near Bethlehem, Pennsylvania, a star is lit in early December and a public service is held in Zinzendorf Square. In Hawaii, under sunny skies, Santa Claus arrives by boat and Christmas dinner is eaten outdoors.

In New Mexico, semi-nomadic Navajo Indians have a 'big feed' at 'Kismus' provided by friends of the Indian peoples. Meat, beans, potatoes and onions are boiled in huge iron pots over campfires. Tubs of coffee with doughnuts, bread and buns complete the menu. In other parts of New Mexico, citizens place luminaires, lighted candles, in paper bags filled with sand. These are put along the streets and on flat roof tops to 'light the way for the Christ Child'.

Immigrant groups of different faiths, holding to the Christmas customs of their homelands, helped to break down Puritan prejudices against Christmas celebrations in America, prejudices which had lasted for over two centuries.

Hessian soldier.

In New England such celebrations had been forbidden by Massachusetts law in 1659 when the General Court decreed:

> *'Anybody who is found observing, by abstinence from labor, feasting, or any other way, any such days as Christmas Day, shall pay for every such offense five shillings.'*

But in New York, Dutch settlers kept a religious and secular holiday period with a mixture of church services, feasting and parties. Of their attitude a writer recorded:

> *'The tranquil, contented burghers were sure to make the most of Christmas-tide, and their neighbors who cursed it must have seemed to them the most whimsical of lunatics.'*

General George Washington took advantage of the German (Hessian) and English troops as they celebrated on December 25, 1776. For on that night the 'rebel' troops of the American Revolution crossed the Delaware River and defeated them at Trenton. Doubtless the Hessians and English soldiers had eaten and drunk too well to keep up their patrols and vigilance! But the Germans triumphed in the end by introducing the Christmas tree, which was set up first in Pennsylvania and spread to other states before Princess Lieven, according to Grenville's *Diary*, brought it to England in 1829. The Pennsylvanian Germans for example have their own *Fur Nicholas* or *Pelznickel*, white-bearded, in old clothes trimmed with fur. He has a bag of toys which he gives to good children, while he taps the naughty ones with his switch. Germans, indeed, can claim to have originated the Christmas tree through the *Paradeisbaum*, the Paradise Tree of German mystery plays. They hung apples on a fir-tree and ringed the tree with lighted candles to represent the fruit and brightness of the Garden of Eden.

English settlers for their part brought the Yule log custom to the U.S. and did their best to introduce the boar's head. Perhaps its academic origins appealed less to American minds than to the dons of Queen's College, Oxford. The legend is that a student of Queen's, attacked by a wild boar on Christmas Day, choked the animal by stuffing a copy of Aristotle down its throat. He thriftily cut off the head to retrieve his Aristotle and carried the head in triumph to the Queen's College High table, where the feast is celebrated each year.

The American custom in some parts of using a small porker is a pale porcine echo of the robust Norse origins of the boar's head custom. Freyr, the god of peace and plenty, used to ride on a boar. Heroes of Valhalla feasted continually on the flesh of boars sacrificed in his honour. The same zest and robustness is reflected in William King's 17th-century *Art of Cookery:*

> '. . . . *send up the Brawner's Head,*
> *Sweet Rosemary and Bays around it spread:*
> *His foaming tusks· let some large Pippin grace,*
> *Or 'midst these thund'ring Spears an Orange place.'*

Most of the seven million Poles, with 600,000 of them in Chicago alone, keep up homeland customs. On Christmas Eve they will spread hay on the floor and under the tablecloth to remind them of an inn or the stable and manger. No meat is eaten that day, but the evening, when the first star appears, ends the fast of *Wigilia*. Beetroot soup, various fish, cabbage, mushrooms and sweetmeats made from honey and poppy seeds are features of the meal.

The master of the house first distributes an *oplatek*, a thin oblong wafer of bread with the Nativity scene imprinted on it. The family and guests wish each other a happy coming year and recall

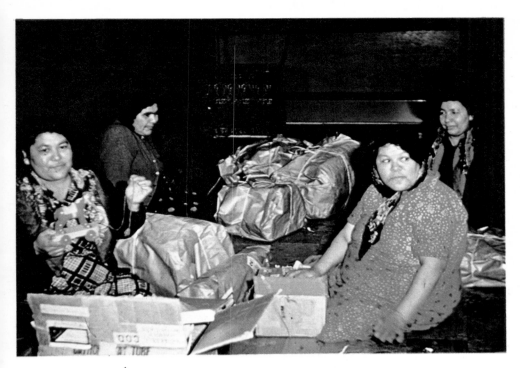

North American Indians wrapping up Christmas parcels.

the birth of Jesus as each member breaks off a piece. An extra place is set at table for Mary and the Christ Child in case they knock at the door of the 'inn' with a request for shelter. In country districts in Poland parts of the wafer were given to the horses and cows.

Poles also stage a puppet play about the Nativity. Its setting is an elaborate construction of gay-coloured turrets and towers, similar to a church, and called a *Szopka*. Children carry this from house to house.

Puerto Ricans, many of them living in difficult conditions in New York City, welcome Santa Claus in his American shape and style. But they do not allow the spiritual meaning of Christmas to be overcoated by materialism. This quality they bring with them from their homeland where January 6, Three Kings' Day, is the main focus of festivities. The Three Kings, dressed in rich costumes, go from house to house where Puerto Ricans live, bringing presents, mainly of fruit.

Children in many of these families are taught to expect gifts, not from Santa Claus, but from the Three Kings. Among the dizzy turrets and concrete ziggurats of New York the children are hardly able to gather the traditional grass from river banks to place under their beds or on the roofs in boxes, as food for the Three Kings' camels. But they still hope the Kings will bring them toys and other gifts.

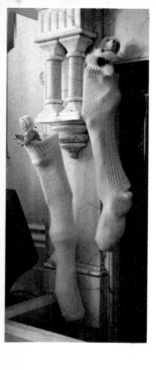

During three open house days, January 6, 7 and 8, men go from house to house playing their guitars. Visitors arrive early in the morning to pay a Christmas call, and the hostess is expected to make up a song on the spot to greet each caller with some suitable words.

'Bethlehem Day', January 12 in Puerto Rico, completes the celebration of Christmas and helps to preserve the real meaning of Christmas. Not easy to perform in city traffic, it consists of three children dressed as Wise Men, leading a procession through the streets. Riding on ponies or horses, they hold gifts for the infant King in their hands. Others dressed as angels, shepherds and flute players follow.

Hungarian Americans place more emphasis on church services and carol-singing on Christmas Eve and Day than many fellow Americans. On Christmas Eve, before the evening meal, the family gathers round their tree and presents are handed out. As in some other East European countries, the appearing of the first star of evening has special importance. After the presents seasonal foods are baked, rolls of walnut and poppy seed, dumplings with honey and poppy seed, and biscuits with caraway, sesame or aniseed.

A heart-warming family time, conscious of a spiritual event, is what means most to Hungarians. They do not go in for funny paper hats and crowns as at some English Christmas parties.

MEXICO

In Mexico, Christmas is not a season for giving presents but for acting out the Christmas story in a popular way. Celebrations start nine days before December 25. These days are called *posadas*, the Spanish for 'lodgings'. The word refers to the inns at which Jesus and Mary stopped on their journey to Bethlehem.

Each night a family gives their home as a *posada* for a festive evening. When darkness falls, processions form led by children. They carry a small litter with statues or clay figures of Mary riding on a donkey, Joseph walking in front and an angel following. Everyone else carries a lighted candle and all join in singing hymns.

The procession halts at a house with a song asking for hospitality for the divine travellers. With a song in reply they are told that the household is asleep. They are threatened with beating if they stay. Then try at other houses till they reach the *posada* which has been chosen in advance. Here they kneel, sing and place the images on a temporary altar decorated with flowers and tapers. After the adoration ceremony the night's celebrations continue with plenty of Mexican refreshments, music and dancing.

Each night of the nine *posadas* a *pinata* or clay jar is broken. This can be a jar of any size, covered with bright-coloured papier-mâché figures such as aeroplanes, birds, animals or even Donald Ducks. It contains sweets and toys. In rich homes, *pinatas* may also hold silk stockings and jewellery.

Children are blindfolded, given a stick and have to find and break a *pinata* which two people hold dangling from a rope. Usually the youngest child is allowed to break it and everybody scrambles for its contents.

On Christmas Eve the images are taken to a crib where the Christ Child is venerated. After Midnight Mass bells are rung, whistles blown and fireworks set off.

Santa Claus in Mexico City.

Music

A literary friend told me that because the ballad of Good King Wenceslas was not of ancient folk origin it was not a "proper" carol. (It was invented by Dr. Neale, a Victorian clergyman and brilliant scholar.) But how old is the tune? Play it with one finger, or on some other instrument than a piano, or just sing it to "Pom-pom-pom", but take it much faster than it is usually sung and get someone to clap loudly or bang a tin on the accents—every second note. It will then sound what it originally was—a dance. That belief cannot be proved with documents because, when it was a dance, only monks and educated people could write music; others carried tunes in their heads and handed them on by singing or playing.

The written tune set to Neale's verses was found in a Swedish book of 1592 called *Piae Cantiones* (Sacred Songs). As in many of Luther's German hymns called chorales, a secular tune had already been slowed down, but set to verses more suitable for Easter than Christmas. You can set it to the English translation *Spring has now unwrapped the flowers* at No. 99 of the Oxford Book of Carols. Is it "a proper carol"? As sung in Sweden it may have sounded more like a hymn.

Yet it is foolish to say "This isn't a proper carol" to every seasonal song that was not originally a *caraula* or singing dance, or to every Christmas favourite that lacks the folk-dance rhythm of *I saw three ships come sailing in* or *Good Christian men rejoice* (a 19th century version of *In dulci jubilo*) or *Masters in this hall* or *Ding dong, merrily on high.* Old and modern manger-crib lullabies, simple songs like *Silent Night* (composed for an Austrian village in 1818), *Away in a manger* (Philadelphia, U.S.A. 1883), *In the bleak midwinter* (words by Christina Rosetti, c. 1885, tunes by Holst, Darke and others) are worth calling carols if only to distinguish them from solid hymns like *While shepherds watched,* the 18th century *O come all ye faithful,* or the chorus from one of Mendelssohn's cantatas which, despite its composer's objections, is now securely married to Wesley's *Hark the herald angels sing.* These grand tunes have qualities other than the lilt of a carol to establish their popularity. It is therefore understandable that more than half the contents of so called carol-sheets, supplied for church, community, domestic or outdoor singing are, in fact, Christmas hymns from standard collections.

Some of our most attractive carols may be older than Christmas or at least older than the keeping of Christmas. Without modern comforts, books, radio, even the means of keeping fresh food from the months of plenty, our forbears needed a cheering break in midwinter. Amid their settlements they kept carnival with communal singing and dancing. They made a big fire and held what we should call a barbecue. This pagan festival was called Yule. We still speak of the Yule log; but the Yule tree, which became the Christmas tree, explains certain old carols.

Our ancestors were wise, for they regarded the sun, rivers and growing things as sources of life. They danced around evergreen trees and plants which did not die in winter, but seemed to be inhabited by living spirits. The well known verses of *The holly and the ivy* which mention neither Christ nor Christmas, belong to the festival of Yule.

The holly and the ivy, when they are both full grown,
Of all the trees that are in the wood the holly bears the crown.
O the rising of the sun and the running of the deer,
The singing of the robin when merry Yule is here!

You probably see that I have cheated, and that the last line should be: *The playing of the merry organ, sweet singing in the choir.* I should like to think that the first Christian missionaries allowed the old festival to continue suitably Christianised, and simply added to or altered the songs. The alterations to *The holly and the ivy* can hardly have been made until at least 1300. Until late in the Middle Ages only royal chapels and monasteries had organs and choirs. Then, after several centuries of the Dark Ages during which church authorities had maintained a puritanical disapproval of public dancing and merrymaking, there began a golden age of carols.

Let us consider the first golden age of the carol. In the Dark Ages, holidays were observed in plenty, although the popular forms of merrymaking (including *caraulae*, singing dances) were despised by the socially or religiously privileged. Carols in the English language and, abroad, in other languages continued; no doubt where words or tunes were in danger of being forgotten locally, the travelling clowns and minstrels revived them on fair grounds and the people took up the choruses; but the fact that they were not written down accounts for differing versions both of words and music. Then, during the thirteenth century a new spirit was born, symbolised by St. Francis of Assisi and his friars (brothers) who called themselves *joculatores Dei* (God's clowns) and travelled to all European countries as evangelists of the poor, using the local languages. They also made use of what we now call "visual aids", especially the models of the Bethlehem Crib and of the Easter Garden. The people themselves made these tableaux, learnt the words of Scripture, and spoke not only single-character words e.g. Joseph's "They have no room at the inn", but also those for groups, such as the shepherds' "Let us now go to Bethlehem" or the Jewish crowd's "Not this man but Barabbas!"

The Oberammergau Passion Play and modern Nativity plays are merely late and often elaborately staged developments of simple presentations of gospel scenes which the friars arranged and encouraged. Almost all could participate, for many characters were

invented. Joseph's neighbours could call at his carpenter's shop and inquire after Mary's health. A village comic could play a silly neighbour, or indeed the part of Herod or Pilate, even the Devil. It was a seriously-taken honour to be the young mother who played Mary, and Francis liked the baby to be a poor orphan, so that those who greeted him at the crib promised that he would be cherished by them. Above all, however, there already existed the music (for players, soloists and all present) in the carols which now came, so to speak, "above ground" . . . not only for Christmas, but for spring and summer festivals and drama. Church authorities could not fail to see that folk were learning Bible truths in their own language when hitherto this had been officially impossible, and that simple peoples' religion was fertilised by the heartfelt use of old carols and the increasing crop of new ones.

During the fifteenth century the larger cities and towns staged the Christmas and other plays magnificently and expensively on big floats like those in carnival processions. These horse-drawn stages were called pagonds (wagons) which gave the name "pageant". They might have several stopping places round the town—the market square, the churchyard gate, an inn yard, a cross roads etc., so that people standing in one place could watch the whole cycle of scenes. If they wished, they could see any scene a second time by following it to another station. Each trade guild took responsibility for a scene, and was proud of its properties, costumes, text and music, including instrumental music. These were preserved and stored, to be used another year unless they could be improved. The pathetic *Coventry Carol* belonged to the scene of Herod's slaughter of the Holy Innocents: the babes of Bethlehem among whom Herod supposed there to be a rival King of Judaea. It was played by the guild of shearmen and tailors.

Yet comedy was also allowed within these religious plays. One most attractive item was the *Donkey Carol* which followed the hissing and booing of King Herod, from whom the Holy Family escaped into Egypt on a donkey. The animal was welcomed and fed

by onlookers to a Latin verse (which suggests educated or trained singers):

Orientis partibus	*From eastern lands*
Adventavit asinus,	*the ass has come,*
Pulcher et fortissimus	*beautiful and very loud,*
Sarcinis aptissimus.	*most worthy of his hay.*

The chorus, however, was in English, for all to join:

Hey, Sir Donkey, Hey (Repeated with hee-haws)

The tune is printed in standard English hymn books. Though still called *Orientis partibus*, it is associated with Easter verses. It is a pity that in older hymn books the tune was deprived of its unison dance-lilt and set to *Christ the Lord is risen today* in solid 4-part harmony and 4/4 time . . . turned from merry carol to solemn hymn.

In England the Reformation did not totally submerge carols. Extremists, as in Switzerland, banned from churches all instrumental and choral music, allowing only the unison singing of metrical psalms. They were unlikely to tolerate reminders of the old plays, holidays and merrymakings. We are fortunate, however, that while the Reformation progressed so did music printing, giving us proof that some of the most attractive popular tunes survived even if some of the words were revised. We see several in the hymn books, choir music and organ albums of music-loving Lutheran Germany, which also printed a rich crop of songs, usually called *Arien*, for the family circle. Choirs are specially grateful for German versions of *In dulci jubilo, Puer natus in Bethlehem*, the carol we sing to the translation *O Little One sweet* and others, which culminate in Bach's fine harmonisations. They remain appealing despite the necessary slowing-down to the contemplative seriousness of hymns. Many of our present carol books would be much the poorer without similar "choir" settings of old carols which have been taken from Swedish, Dutch and Czech collections.

Evidently Catholic France enjoyed merry carols at Christmas without the hymn-like treatment. Whether they were ever sung during junctures of the liturgy we do not know, but we have delicious variations on "Noëls" by French organists (some of them royal organists) of the seventeenth and eighteenth centuries. The best are those by Dandrieu, Clérambault, Le Bègue and Daquin.

What about carols in Britain after the Reformation? We cannot tell exactly what was sung after the Reformation in English ordinary churches which had to use the rites approved by governments and printed in the Book of Common Prayer; we only know that the Elizabethan injunctions allowed "a hymn or such like song" at a juncture in the service, but that after the banishment of music from churches by the Puritan government, "such like songs" came invariably from the collections of metrical psalms from which so many hymns still remain. At the end of these collections we sometimes find "Christmas Hymn" and "Easter Hymn"—the former usually *While shepherds watched*—but never "Christmas Carol". If, however, carol singing had not continued in homes and by waits (wandering or visiting singers), they could not have been recalled for collectors of the second golden age. As in Germany, after the Reformation, there was a demand for songs and part-songs for domestic use, and it seems hardly credible that Byrd wrote his lovely *Lullaby, my sweet little baby* only for Catholic aristocrats among his patrons; yet it is unlikely that, as today, it was sung in cathedrals or even royal chapels.

Popular carols *were* printed—on broadsheets sold at fairs, just as were accounts of murders. The carols mentioned in essays and novels of the 18th and 19th century (usually referring to time past), rarely suggest great merriment, but tend to be staid and moralistic. The favourite of the church-gallery players and singers in Thomas Hardy's *Far from the Madding Crowd* (who went round with it as "waits" at various houses) was *Remember O thou Man, thy time is short.* Dickens mentions the London favourite of his time, *God rest you merry,* but that also is in a minor key. The pity is that even today it is still sung too slowly. Even Methodist collections, with plenty of jolly "human" hymns, lack evidence that old carols were included during their services and meetings; but early in .the 19th century antiquarian scholars began a rescue and published the words of carols and old ballads. Their sources were country singers and broadsheets.

Naturally such folk verses appealed to friends of the romantic literary movement, and although the new "high church" clergy of the 1830s onwards were in a sense ecclesiastical romantics, they were not alone in wishing to bring colour, romance, decoration, fresh music, even pictures and Christmas trees into a religion that was cold and moribund.

Many Victorian musicians and clergy were scholars who were keen to revive old beauty in much the same way as were the later collectors of folk dance and song who were (in Vaughan Williams' words) "only just in time to discover old folk who remembered their treasure". Moreover they, and those who followed them in the work (e.g. Woodward of the *Cowley Carol Book*) did not confine their interest to English materials, but either themselves or from friends, supplied words which have enabled the choicest carols from France, Picardy, Holland, Russia, Spain, Germany, Scandinavia and even American Indian tribes to be sung. The enormous number of carols available to us is enough proof that this little festive form, as well as far from "little" treatments by modern composers, is enjoying a new golden age. Yet one more important contribution to its coming must be mentioned.

In 1887 Edward White Benson became the first bishop of the new diocese of Truro in England, leaving it to become Archbishop of Canterbury in 1883. For Truro he devised a service of readings interspersed by carols for the choir (with one or two Christmas hymns for all to join) which became specially popular when it spread to the college chapels of his old university, Cambridge. How many people have increased their knowledge and repertory of carols, not just those of English provenance, after hearing the broadcasts of that service, year by year, from King's College? When it was first held, how many, even among musicians, knew the Czech *Rocking* and *From out of a wood did a cuckoo fly*, the Dutch *Lord Jesus hath a garden*, the Austrian *He smiles within his cradle*, the Besançon *Chantons bargiés* (sung both to *Shepherds shake off your drowsy sleep* and *People look east*), or even such English carols as *Ding dong* and *Past three o'clock*? The collecting and arranging shows no sign of dwindling, and music directors marvel at the number of carols advertised year by year just before Christmas.

These are not merely new settings and arrangements of old words or tunes by modern composers, but perennial discoveries of old tunes long beloved in Asia, Africa and the Americas as well as Europe and now made available in English versions.

These my friend would call "proper carols", but I find it as hard to define "proper" as to answer my own question: What is a carol? The easy but not quite satisfactory answer is: "When it is a hymn", since in our time the hymn books include more merry-sounding items than they once did, and at certain junctures of the solemn Christmas liturgies (services with a fixed and dignified order), carols provide a variety that does not seem out of place. My own decision as to what is a carol and what is a hymn comes purely from my personal impression. The words: "God of God, Light of Light, lo he abhors not the Virgin's womb! Very God, begotten not created. . ." are distinctly doctrinal, and quote both *Credo* and *Te Deum*; they are not the spontaneous-sounding product of popular rejoicing. They are none the worse for that, nor for being translated from the Latin; but their grand tune *Adeste fideles* loses its grandeur if not sung slowly enough to be impressively solemn, and it loses a good deal without the inclusion of altos, tenors, basses and a fine accompanying instrument. Very different are Christmas pieces that sound well with nothing but their tunes sung by children or played on recorders, e.g. *I saw three ships*, or *Il est né, le divin enfant*. Let each of us answer the question for himself or herself, provided it does not make us exclude excellent seasonal songs as "not *proper* carols"!

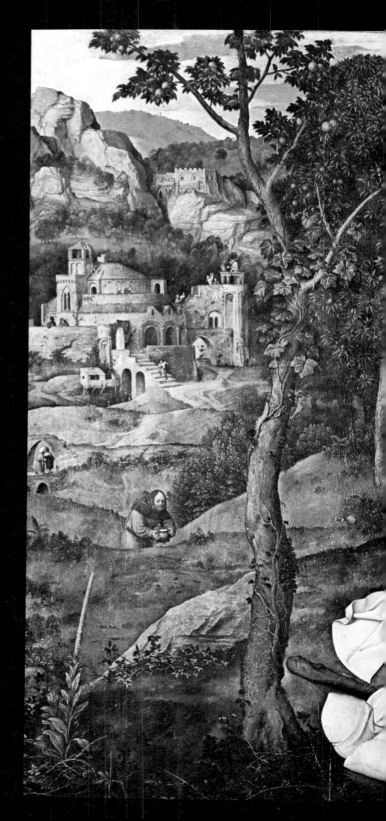

Rest on the Flight into Egypt. Joachim Patenier.

Paintings

'And it came to pass in those days, that there went out a decree from Caesar Augustus, that all the world should be taxed.'

With these rather spare words, the second chapter of St. Luke's Gospel begins the account of the birth of Christ. The story is told in only two of the Gospels, Matthew and Luke, and both are brief, Matthew particularly so. Between them, however, Matthew and Luke provide the foundation from which artists over nearly 1,700 years have created the imagery of the Nativity with which we are now so familiar. There is no colourful background detail in either Gospel version; each verse contributes directly to the main stream of the story, and so leaves ample scope for additional embellishment to be given by others both in pictorial and written form.

Perhaps the most famous addition to the Gospel accounts is the inclusion of the ox and the ass by the manger during the Nativity. Neither Matthew nor Luke mentions them, and the first account in which they appear is the Gospel of Pseudo-Matthew, one of the many apocryphal versions of the Gospels, thought to have been written in the 8th century. Here, in fulfilment of the prophesies of Isaiah and Habakkuk, the ox and the ass are described as adoring the Child as He lies in the manger. This is not a particularly startling addition to the story, because where there was a manger an ox and an ass could hardly be far away, and it is an addition that has become common currency in representations of the Nativity from enormous baroque altarpieces to humble cribs in churches at Christmas. There are many other additional details in Nativity paintings which descend variously from legend, Old Testament prophecy and Christian doctrine, and we shall look at some of these when we see how painters of all periods have depicted the Christmas story from the Annunciation to the Flight into Egypt.

A pictorial problem which all artists painting the Annunciation have to overcome is how to paint an expressive *gap*. The subject calls for two figures meeting—yet not touching—and for the passing from one to the other of a simple but profound message: 'And, behold, thou shalt conceive in thy womb, and bring forth a son, and shalt call his name Jesus' (Luke 1:31). Paradoxically, the gap between the two figures of the Archangel Gabriel and Mary is the crucial part of the composition, because it is through that space that the holy message is passing. The space between them will ideally contain objects or shapes which will help carry the eye gently across it from Gabriel to Mary. The Siennese painter Simone Martini (1284-1344) partially solved the problem in his painting of the *Annunciation* (in the Uffizi Gallery, Florence) by incorporating part of the Latin text of Gabriel's message into the painting, using it literally to bridge the gap between Gabriel's lips and Mary. A vase of white lilies, the symbol of the Virgin's purity, and an indication that the Annunciation took place in the spring, is also placed between the figures.

A wide gap separates the figures in the *Annunciation* painted in about 1445 by Domenico Veneziano (Fitzwilliam Museum, Cambridge). This effortlessly cool painting, with its interplay of soft tones of grey and pink, shows Gabriel kneeling, pointing to heaven, and looking towards Mary who stands on the opposite side

The Annunciation. Domenico Veneziano.

of the courtyard with her head slightly bowed and her arms crossed over her breast. The meeting is shown inside Mary's home, where the measured rhythm of the columns and windows around the courtyard articulate the space behind and between the figures. The otherwise severe verticals and horizontals of the architecture are broken by the diagonals of Gabriel's kneeling body and of his spray of lilies; and another interlude is given to the eye with the glimpse through the archway into the enchanting enclosed garden behind. The presence of the garden gives the eye movement into as well as across the painting, and allows a subtle contrast between the riot of flowers over the bower and the formality of the architecture in the foreground. The door in the garden wall is firmly bolted from the inside, thus creating a *hortus conclusus* ('enclosed garden'). This is a symbol borrowed from the Old Testament Song of Solomon (4:12): 'A garden inclosed is my sister, my spouse; a spring shut up, a fountain sealed', which was taken from the Middle Ages to represent Mary's virginity. So in a very quiet, understated way Domenico Veneziano has pointed out how central Mary's virginity is to her Annunciation.

A painting of the Annunciation made more than 450 years before the version by Domenico Veneziano is included in the *Codex Egberti* (Trier, Stadtbibliothek), a manuscript completed around 983 containing illustrations and texts from the Gospels. The manuscript was made for Egbert, Archbishop of Trier, a town situated in what is now West Germany, a few miles from the border with Luxembourg. The artist's name is not known for certain, so he is called the Master of the *Registrum Gregorii*, after another of his most famous works (see illustration on page 88).

Although we do not know his name, we do know that the Master of the *Registrum Gregorii* must have been a very well-travelled man with an extensive knowledge of the surviving examples of the 4th- and 5th-century pagan Roman art (the period generally known as 'late antique'), and it has been suggested that he came from Italy. This is significant, because the figures in his *Annunciation* (as in other examples of his work) have a strongly classical appearance, and are probably based on figures in a now unknown 4th- or 5th-century Roman manuscript. A clue to the classical origin of the figures lies in the draperies, which hang in wide folds about the figures in a manner closely reminiscent of statues of important Romans. This is particularly clear in the figure of Gabriel, who, without his wings, cross, halo and somewhat naïvely eager expression, could so easily be a Roman orator grandly making a point in the Senate.

This *Annunciation* differs in many obvious respects from the version by Domenico Veneziano, but perhaps the fundamental difference lies in the composition. The figures in the Domenico are widely separated in cool architectural surroundings, whereas the figures in the *Codex Egberti Annunciation* are standing close together outside the (helpfully labelled) City of Nazareth. The city is shown merely as a symbol, upon an equally symbolic hill, and is composed of buildings which seem barely able to stay squeezed within the confines of the city wall. The artist has taken literally the verse in St. Luke's Gospel (1:26): 'And in the sixth month the angel Gabriel was sent from God unto a city of Galilee, named Nazareth'; but in placing the figures outside the city has not taken up one of the levels of meaning that follows in verse 28 ('And the angel came *in* unto her . . .') that the Annunciation took place in Mary's home. There is little expressiveness in the gap between the figures; no electric force seems to flow between them as it does between the protagonists in the Domenico *Annunciation*. The painting does reflect, however, through the monumental and superhuman appearance of the figures, the Holy Roman Emperor-centred society for which it was commissioned.

Opposite: '*Ecce Ancilla Domini*'. Rossetti.

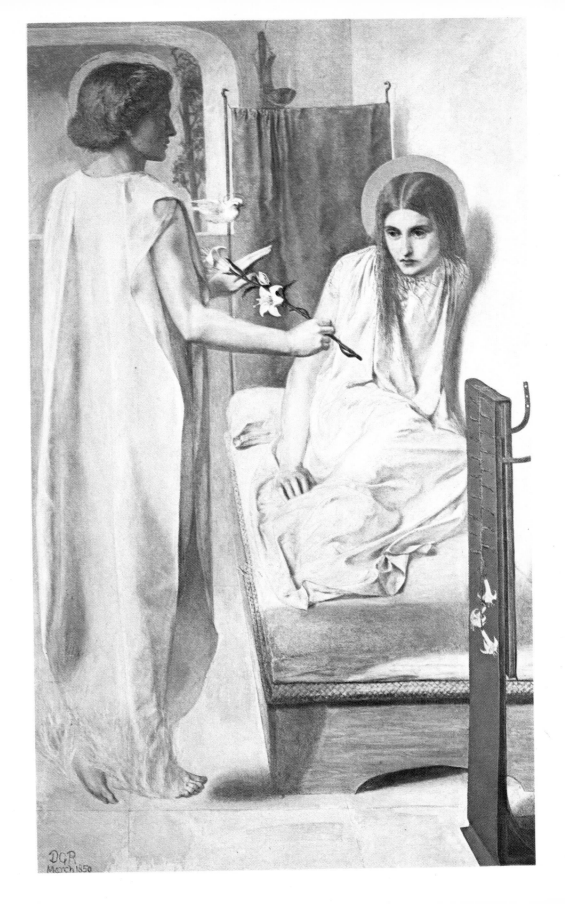

Dante Gabriel Rossetti's painting of the *Annunciation,* in the Tate Gallery, London, made in 1850, shows Mary to have a most human reaction to Gabriel's unexpected and disturbing visit. She does not react submissively like Domenico Veneziano's Virgin, but shrinks startled towards the wall of her narrow room, as, no doubt, one would. Mary herself is a perfectly real sort of person, a type we know we have met somewhere, and is in fact a portrait of Rossetti's younger sister, Christina. The gap between the figures is closed by the scene being set on the diagonal, and this adds a claustrophobic effect to the ascetic line and colouring. The alternative title to the painting is *'Ecce Ancilla Domini'*—'Behold the handmaid of the Lord' (Luke 1:38), and Rossetti shows the handmaid accepting her duty with the greatest humility.

Where the Archangel Gabriel and Mary must not touch in paintings of the Annunciation, the figures in the scene which immediately follows it in Luke's Gospel, the Visitation, are generally depicted as embracing or clasping hands. Luke tells (1:39-56) how, after Gabriel's visit, Mary hurries into the hills of Judea to the home of her cousin Elisabeth. Elisabeth is also pregnant, expecting her son John, who is later to become John the Baptist. Elisabeth was the first to perceive the true nature of Jesus, and says to Mary: 'Blessed art thou among women, and blessed is the fruit of thy womb. And whence is this to me that the mother of my Lord should come to me? For, lo, as soon as the voice of thy salutation sounded in mine ears, the babe leaped in my womb for joy.' The German painter Marx Reichlich (1460—after 1520) made a painting of the *Visitation* in 1511 as part of an altarpiece which is now in the Alte Pinakothek in Munich. Mary has just arrived at Elisabeth's home (which is indeed shown to be in 'hill country'), and as the two cousins meet we can actually see how Elisabeth's baby 'Leaped in her womb'. The foetal John the Baptist is shown already to be kneeling before the foetal Jesus who in turn gives John his blessing. This charming detail is one which first appeared in 5th- or 6th-century Byzantine painting, and which spread to the West in paintings of the Annunciation and Visitation. It is seen particularly in German painting up to the 15th century, when with rare exceptions it died out, and is typical of the mystical and symbolic way in which northern European artists portrayed the story of the nativity in the 15th century.

In the second chapter of his gospel, Luke tells of the birth of Jesus (verse 7): 'And she brought forth her firstborn son, and wrapped him in swaddling clothes, and laid him in a manger; because there was no room for them in the inn.' These few simple words have been the inspiration for some of the most moving paintings in the history of art, and any small selection of them is bound to reflect a personal taste. The Nativity is often represented at night, especially when combined with the Adoration of the

The Nativity. The Paum Gartner Altar Piece.

Shepherds, and this gives scope for artists to create mysterious effects of strong light and shadow within a dark gloomy stable. *The Nativity at Night* (National Gallery, London), ascribed to the late 15th-century Netherlandish painter Geertgen tot Sint Jans (his name means 'The Little Gerard of the Brethren of St. John'), shows the inner light of a doll-like Jesus illuminating brightly the wondering faces around him. The light also picks out the beams and broken walls of the stable, and is the brightest of three separate sources of illumination in the painting. The other two sources are in the background, where an angel rushes towards the shepherds and lights up the hillside, completely outfacing the third source, the feeble little earthly light given out by the shepherds' camp-fire. Thus, the heavenly light of Christ is shown symbolically to be of greater power than the light of angels and of men.

Although many Nativity paintings, like Geertgen's, incorporate the scene of the Annunciation to the shepherds in the background, Luke's description of the angels telling the shepherds of Christ's birth (2:8-14) contains sufficient imagery to make it a subject in its own right. A drawing by William Blake (1757-1827) of the *Shepherds and the Choir of Angels* (Whitworth Art Gallery, Manchester), c. 1809, follows Luke's report of the scene, but more specifically illustrates it from a verse in *Hymn on the Morning of Christ's Nativity* by John Milton:

> **At last surrounds their sight**
> **A Globe of circular light,**
> **That with long beams the shame-fac't night array'd,**
> **The helmèd Cherubim**
> **And sworded Seraphim,**
> **Are seen in glittering ranks with wings displayed,**
> **Harping in loud and solemn quire,**
> **With unexpressive notes to Heaven's new-born Heir.**

A *Nativity* by a modern artist which is nevertheless very much in the 15th-century Netherlandish tradition is by the English painter Charles Mahoney (1903-1968). The scene is again set at night, on an ivy patch at the bottom of an English garden, and shows the shepherds coming rather nervously to worship the Child. Two of them are dressed in heavy great-coats (apparently ex-Army), and also wear thick mufflers and waistcoats to keep out the winter air. Although all the figures in the painting are solidly formed, there still seems to be an air of unreality around Mary and the Child, with which the shepherds are finding it hard to come to terms. In front of the painting are two girls with long-bobbed hair kneeling in prayer, and the work as a whole has the open, democratic feeling which is present in Nativity and Adoration paintings by 15th-century Netherlandish and German artists such as Hugo van de Goes, Hans Memlinc, Gerard David, Geertgen and Dürer.

The painting by Geertgen is one with an intensely private appeal, and is of a small scale which fitted it as an aid for private contemplation and worship. A painting of exactly the same subject, but made for quite a different purpose, is the *Adoration of the Shepherds* (1638, Musée des Beaux-Arts, Grenoble) by the Spanish painter Francisco Zurbaran (1598-1664). It is a large work (2.61 m. $\times$ 1.75 m.) intended to be seen by large numbers of people, and to convince them (if they needed to be convinced) of the divine significance of the birth of Christ. To emphasise the holiness of the event, Zurbaran has painted a view into Heaven itself, making it into a physical presence in the painting peopled by dumpy young cherubs who are as real as the rough-skinned Spanish peasants who worship the Child below. The work is a product of the Counter-Reformation period of the 16th and 17th centuries, which began to have an effect on painting and sculpture after the Council of Trent in 1563. Disturbed by the successes of the Protestant reformers who tended to think that all art was idolatrous, the leaders of the Roman Catholic Church dictated that paintings and sculptures were a positive aid to worship, because through them the faithful could be reminded of the lives of Christ and the saints and of their miracles. Although the most powerful aspect of the Zurbaran is the combination of the equally real earthly and heavenly figures, there is also a certain amount of the symbolism which is traditional to Nativity paintings of all ages. On the right is a sheep with its legs tied, a gift to the Child from the shepherds, representing Christ's future sacrifice. The eggs brought in a basket by the girl on the left symbolise the Resurrection, and the fragments of a classical column among the ruins shows how the Christian era, just beginning with the Nativity, supersedes decaying paganism.

The Flight into Egypt. Fra Angelico.

85

The Holy Family on the Steps. Poussin.

The Geertgen, Mahoney and Reni are all informal paintings which seem to embrace the viewer and draw him closer into the scene. The same happily accessible and very human feeling is present in *The Holy Family* (see page 90) by the Spaniard Bartolomé Esteban Murillo (1618-82) in the Prado, Madrid. This could be any family in their own home, and there are no immediately apparent religious overtones. Because of this, it is diametrically opposed to another *Holy Family* group painted at almost the same time, 1648, by the French painter Nicholas Poussin (1594-1665). This is *The Holy Family on the Steps* in the National Gallery of Art, Washington, which has a rigid and monarchical appearance making it

apparent that the spectator can only view the group at a distance. Not only does the perspective seem to set them above our eye-level, but the rigidly planned and somewhat forbidding architecture emphasises the hieratic arrangement of the figures. Although we can gaze in awe on the figures, none of them returns our gaze, and only Mary is actually looking out of the painting, slightly to the left. The passing of the apple from the young St. John to Jesus, however, is of much greater symbolic importance than any eye-contact between the figures and the viewer, because, when it is shown in Christ's hands, the apple represents the fruit of salvation. As if re-enacting the Fall, when Eve gave the apple to Adam, the young St. John is handing the apple to Christ, the new Adam. The interpretation of the apple as a symbol of Christ comes from the Song of Solomon, 2:3: 'As the apple tree among the trees of the wood, so is my beloved among the sons. I sat down under his shadow with great delight, and his fruit was sweet to my taste.'

St. Matthew is the only Evangelist who tells of the visit of the Magi. Matthew 2:11 reads: 'And when they were come into the house, they saw the young child with Mary his mother, and fell down, and worshipped him: and when they had opened their treasures, they presented unto him gifts; gold, and frankincense, and myrrh.'

Where the subject of the *Adoration of the Shepherds* can be happily interpreted in small-scale, intimate paintings, such as Geertgen tot Sint Jans' *Nativity, at Night*, the *Adoration of the Magi* is a subject that lends itself to grand pictures, loaded with colour, pomp and circumstance, and the additional humbling contrast with the poverty of the stable and the richness of the spirit of Mary, Jesus and Joseph. One of the grandest and greatest paintings of *The Adoration of the Magi* was made in 1624 by the Flemish artist Peter Paul Rubens (1577-1640). It hangs in the Musée Royale des Beaux Arts in Antwerp, and a smaller study for it is in the Wallace Collection in London. Immediately one is aware of the enormous, richly dressed figures filling and overflowing from the stable, and paying homage to the small, wriggling child on the right. The contrast between the two groups is staggering, but Rubens has composed the painting so that the great descending curve of figures from the top right to bottom centre frames, halts before and emphasises the figures of Mary and Jesus.

The Adoration of the Magi (c. 1506/07) by the Venetian painter Giorgione (1477-1510) in the National Gallery, London, is a tiny picture by comparison to the Rubens (the Rubens is 4.47 m. × 2.35 m. while the Giorgione is only 0.29 m. × 0.81 m.). Its proportions suggest that it was painted as a predella to an altarpiece—that is as a small panel fixed along the bottom edge of the larger main painting. The difference between the Rubens and the Giorgione is not only one of scale: Giorgione's *Adoration* is a

Christmas

much less grand occasion. The simple, but wonderfully sculptural, figures of Mary, Joseph and Jesus sit beside the stable while they are approached by the kings and their rather worldly courtiers wearing the latest Venetian fashions. It is a meeting of two worlds: the secular paying homage to the sacred.

The Annunciation in the Codex Egberti. Master of the Registrum Gregorii.

Opposite: *The Nativity at Night. Geertgen.*

There is just a hint that some of the courtiers in the Giorgione see this as a rather boring day out. The *Adoration of the Magi* (1423) by the Italian Gentile da Fabriano (*c.* 1360-*c.* 1427) in the Uffizi in Florence shows, on the other hand, the event as an exciting and highly fashionable excursion. The three kings themselves are almost lost before the crowds of their supporters, who bring along their horses, dogs, hawks, monkeys and even a leopard, enjoying the occasion hugely. This *Adoration* is painted in the International Gothic style which had its roots in Germany and France but which, as its name suggests, was practised by artists all over western Europe between the 13th and the 15th centuries. Its characteristics are plainly apparent in Gentile's painting: intense and loving naturalistic detail in plants, animals, rocks, costumes and figures, and the consequent use of bright colours and gold, and a mass of life and movement.

The traditional iconography of the *Rest on the Flight to Egypt* has some similarities with the Nativity itself, although there is no stable or ox, and the family are shown in an oasis, or other lush spot. Mary has the Child on her lap or at her breast, and Joseph is with the ass nearby either working in the fields, collecting food for the family to eat, or just lying, exhausted by the journey. St. Matthew's Gospel tells why the family fled to Egypt (2:13): 'And when they [the Wise Men] were departed, behold, the angel of the Lord appeareth to Joseph in a dream, saying, Arise, and take the young child and his mother, and flèe into Egypt, and be thou there until I bring thee word: for Herod will seek the young child to destroy him.' In the painting of the *Rest on the Flight* by the early Netherlandish artist Joachim Patenier (active 1515-1524) in the Prado, Madrid, we see Mary suckling the Child in the foreground, with Joseph climbing the slope on the left carrying a bowl. On the right is the ass grazing, while in the background are some soldiers talking to men cutting corn. This detail is drawn from apocryphal legend, in which during the journey to Egypt the Holy Family met a labourer who was sowing wheat. The story goes that Jesus put His hand into the sack and threw a handful of seed onto the ground, and immediately the wheat grew until it was as large and as ripe as it would be if it had been growing for a year. When Herod's soldiers came up to the labourer, they asked him if he had seen a woman carrying a child. When he replied, quite truthfully, 'Yes, when I was sowing my corn', the soldiers assumed that he was talking about a woman and child who had passed by a year ago. Thinking the labourer to be a little crazy, the soldiers turned back no doubt to join their friends massacring the innocents in the village in the background of the painting.

A picture that gives a very real feeling of fatigue to the figures is *The Rest on the Flight to Egypt* by the Italian painter Orazio Gentileschi (*c.* 1563-1639) in Birmingham City Museum and Art

ie *Holy Family. Bartolomé* teban *Murillo.*

The Rest on the Flight to Egypt. Orazio Gentileschi.

Gallery. Joseph in particular is exhausted, while Mary seems only just able to summon up enough energy to feed the Child. Behind them the head of their donkey emerges surrealistically from behind a brick wall, and seems to float in weird disembodied profile in front of a steely grey sky. This is a remarkable, if somewhat bizarre interpretation of the subject, and is one which Gentileschi repeated with variations at least four times. The painting in Birmingham is now accepted to be his first version, painted in Italy before Gentileschi arrived in England in 1626 to become court painter to King Charles I. Where it differs from more traditional representations of the subject is in the very stark composition with the figures cut off from surrounding life and landscape by the dominating and imprisoning brick wall. As if as a result of this isolation from the world, Gentileschi makes Mary and Joseph show little warmth or human feeling for the Child, and has created a disturbing and even horrific picture of the event.

The Flight into Egypt (1609) by the German Adam Elsheimer (1578-1610) in the Alte Pinakothek, Munich, has the warmth and human feeling that is lacking in the Gentileschi, and a naturalism in the light, darkness and landscape that is not present in Geertgen's much more purist *Nativity at Night* painted perhaps 150 years before. What it shares with the Geertgen, however, is an intimate scale (the Elsheimer, an oil painting on copper, is only 0.31 m.×0.41 m.), and a feeling of mystery in the way it is lit. But whereas the light effect in Geertgen's painting is unreal, and is clearly a vehicle to convey the message of the spiritual nature of Christ, Elsheimer lights the landscape for the first time in the history of painting with a closely observed universe of moon and stars. Although their relative sizes and positions are not depicted accurately, Elsheimer has correctly recorded the formation of individual constellations. Reading from left to right, we see the Pleiades, the Milky Way, the constellation Leo, the Great Bear and Arcturus, and from this scholars have inclined to the opinion that Elsheimer was aware of contemporary developments in astronomy leading up to the discoveries of Galileo in 1610.

This little landscape, whose composition is united in an uninterrupted sweep from the foreground plants to the furthest constellation, was of seminal influence in European art, and in particular on Rembrandt, Rubens and Inigo Jones. The Holy Family, whose way is lit not by a heavenly light but by the feeble earthly light of a torch, approach an already blazing campfire, which shoots an exalting shower of sparks to rival the Milky Way. From the evening chill the family is approaching warmth and rest.

Adoration of the Magi. Gentile da Fabriano.

Crafts

Whenever there is a
reason for festivity, whether it is a
family, national or worldwide occasion,
extra special decorations are called for.
Christmas, perhaps the most important
event of all, has tradition deeply
involved with decoration. Many objects
are made only for that occasion,
and stored carefully during the
intervening period. As part of childhood
memories there were those familiar
items which appeared annually
to join the decorations—the angel
for the top of the tree, baubles and glass
icicles or bells and elaborate paper
chains. So although Christmas time
is an invitation to make beautiful
new decorations, it is also steeped
in memory as the old favourites
show their faces for another year.

Decorations receive various
emphasis according to different
nationalities. Whenever the
season is being celebrated, the Nativity
scene should be of prime importance
since it depicts the birthday of Christ.

Children making a crib.

Most churches and schools present the scene of the birth of
Jesus in the form of a 'crib', in which the characters of Mary,
Joseph, the Babe, angels, shepherds and wise men are represented
by three-dimensional figures. This custom was not unknown in
Roman times when dolls and effigies were often displayed at
festivals. The beautiful crib of St. Francis of Assisi in the 13th
century was probably the most striking, since real animals and
people took part in presenting the Nativity scene. Made in many
materials, this scene can be charmingly simple when re-created in
real straw with statuettes; the whole intimate picture telling the
story of Christmas at a glance.

The tradition of Christmas must include the Christmas tree
with its own particular place in the festive decorations. Usually a
simple little fir tree, it stands happily displaying coloured lights,

outside or indoors, heavily festooned with tinsel, parcels and other decorations. Some of these take the form of cookies and other carefully shaped edible goodies. In European countries this delightful custom transforms the tree, whilst in America and England the decorations glitter far more with tinsel and baubles. The trees of our forefathers would have been decorated with candles and tiny parcels dangling from the branches. Our electric lights are certainly a safer substitute.

Christmas, it should be remembered, is not always celebrated in the dark and the snow, as, particularly in the Southern Hemisphere, Christmas Day itself may well be brilliantly sunny and is celebrated by a picnic on the beach. Therefore the temptation to involve too much tinsel and glitter should perhaps be resisted. However, where it enhances the marvellous range of natural materials it can be a charming, glittering addition. With the planning and preparations involved, one must take advantage of traditional Christmas cones and evergreens in the areas where trees are plentiful. In Scandinavia the finery of wooden handicrafts, such as shaving strips with wooden beads or straw stars, is amongst the most delightful and refined decorations. Other materials like paper, glass and foil or candles combine beautifully with these.

It is easy to see how the traditional colours have become established. Red, the warm, comforting glow, the colour of Santa Claus' cloak, the colour of holly berries. Not, as one would imagine, from the robin, the little red-breasted bird, but from the first postmen, dressed in red, who were called robins. In turn it is the little bird that has earned a significant inclusion in Christmas. White, the crisp, frosty snow, the sparkling lights of the star and candles. Silver and gold simply emphasise the reflections. Green the Christmas tree and other evergreens.

Most of all, the holly has all these colours and has become the most significant of Christmas plant material. The use of much of this evergreen material may well have pre-Christmas origins. Holly may well have been a holy tree, reminding us of new life in its evergreen leaves, as well as reflecting on the prickly leaves as a reminder of the thorns in the crown which this same Jesus was to wear some thirty years later. The red berries also serve to tell us of the blood He was to shed. A reminder of Good Friday even amid the joy of Christmas. Mistletoe has its origin as a decorative item in pre-Christian days. It appears that in Norse legend Loki, the evil god, made an arrow of the poisonous wood of a mistletoe branch which he used to kill Balder, the sun god. The other gods brought Balder back to life and the mistletoe tree promised never to harm again, but rather to become a symbol of love. Perhaps that is why we now use mistletoe as an excuse for kissing.

The spruce or fir tree has not always been recognised as the Christmas tree. There is a record that in 1605 at Christmas time in Strasbourg fir trees were taken into houses and decorated with coloured paper, gold foil and sweets, but this custom was not introduced into England until the 19th century when it was popularised by Queen Victoria's husband, Prince Albert. Queen Elizabeth still gives two trees each Christmas to the Dean of St. Paul's to display in the cathedral, but the large one given to London by the people of Oslo each year is better known.

The Christmas tree, whether large or small, commands the centre of attention and is an invitation to the whole family to make decorations for it. The shapes of the decorations fall into two basic patterns, the pendant or the streamer. Most important of all is the very top, which either has a simple star, like the one over the stable at Bethlehem, or a fairy doll. It is possible to make a star in several ways. A straw star can be made by soaking straws and tying them into shape before they are left to dry. It can then be sprayed with silver paint, or just left plain (see colour illustration). Alternatively, a cardboard star can be cut out and covered with aluminium foil.

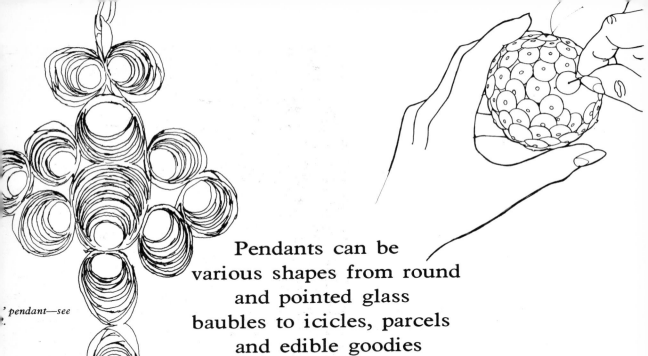

pendant—see

Pendants can be
various shapes from round
and pointed glass
baubles to icicles, parcels
and edible goodies
to little snowmen, angels
and figures of
Santa Claus.

The glass baubles vary from clear crystal
and plain metallic colours to decorated ones.
Some of these decorations are simply painted
with patterns and glitter, while others can
be elaborately covered with scenes of
intricate detail.

The simplest of these to decorate are the plain
glass spheres which can be painted with
glue and then dipped in glitter. Individual
baubles with names painted on them are a
novel idea. These glass decorations are
made in a variety of shapes and can be
imitated with other materials. Spheres
made by pushing beads and sequins into
polystyrene shapes can provide endless
entertainment for adults and children alike.
The patterns, whether intricate or
simple, can be individual pieces of work with
lace and ribbon, held in place with the pins.
Several beads on a pin will create an antenna
and a combination of these with flat sequins
produce an object appearing to be
from outer space.

Tiny statuettes can be made to dangle from the tree. Using the polystyrene ball as a base, a clown's head can be very simply made by pinning eyes, nose and mouth with sequins, giving him a pointed hat with a frill for his neck. Snowmen are symbolic of Christmas and a visit to the wood or forest should produce fir-cones, which make excellent objects for the body. Paint them lightly with colour and dip them in glitter, stick sequins on one to form the face and glue the two cones together end to end. Make a little black paper top hat, then dangle the finished figure from a gold thread used for parcel wrapping. Santa Claus can be made in a similar way, only, of course, red paper should be used for a little cloak and hood. Don't forget his beard which should be a tiny piece of cotton wool. There are birds and all manner of other creatures that can be made, but the most enchanting are the angels. A whole tree decorated with little swinging angels can be quite charming, particularly if accompanied by white lights. There are many different designs and materials to use, but white cartridge paper is one of the easiest to obtain. Very crisp to use, angels made with clear white paper are well displayed against the deep green of the Christmas tree. Made from a basic paper shape, the angel simply slots together and the face and other details are painted afterwards.

Parcels are always intriguing whether they are simply or elaborately wrapped. The contents should be kept as light as possible, so as not to weigh the branches too heavily and distort the shape of the tree. Varying shapes are an asset; in particular a pen or pencil when wrapped can hang as an icicle, and so on.

The long pointed vertical shape adds variation to the baubles and statuettes. Simple strings of metallic beads bunched together rather like catkins are very easy to make and are very popular with industrious children. They can be hooked over the branches and arranged to hang downwards. Ribbon ringlets can also be made to dangle from the tree. A piece of ribbon can be pulled over the blade of a knife to produce a tight spiral, and the process repeated several times to create the right shape. If metallic ribbon is used it will catch the light as the little springs dance between the branches.

Tinsel is a traditional form of streamer to be entwined between the layers. Used for decoration it can enhance or ruin the appearance of the tree. It should be used conservatively and shaped as though it is heavily draped. Also remember to use some in the centre of the tree rather than round the tips of the branches, which may result in it appearing to be trapped in a cobweb of silver rope. Homemade streamers generally are too cumbersome for tree decorations, but, using parcel ribbon, it is possible to make small ones. Choose two colours and fold them over each other alternately, until the required length is achieved. Secure with a little glue to stop the ends from unfolding.

Parcel ribbon is a very adaptable material to use, not only for decorative bows but for tree pendants. Available in a large range of colours, their inclusion is inviting. Circles, like quilling, can be assembled and stapled together or wetted if it is the self-adhesive type. Rosettes are often used for parcels and two joined back to back can make a simple type of pendant. They are effective when made with two contrasting ribbons as the loops display both colours.

There is hardly need to explain why we use candles so extensively at Christmas. In pre-Christian times they represented the heat and light of the sun, which in successive days after Christmas was to increase in strength, while Christians see the candle as a symbol of Jesus, the sun and light of the world. Candles are also symbols of the truth. However, the little flame dancing on the top of a column of wax cannot be surpassed for creating a cosy, intimate atmosphere. Most of all, the light it produces is warm and welcoming, and therefore it deserves to play a large part in Christmas decorations. From a single light to a host of candles, every home can have a welcome with candlelight at Christmas.

Some of the early trees were decorated with candles, and it is easy to imagine how dangerous this can be. In fact, before any decoration is embarked upon, it is essential to fix the candle securely to whatever stand is being used. For example, cork or bark of any type could well be drilled so that the candle can stand in a hole. In some cases a long nail from the underside could pierce the

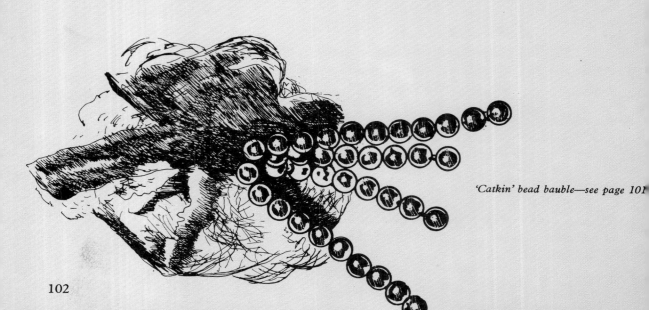

'Catkin' bead bauble—see page 101

candle. Candlesticks quite naturally are designed for the purpose, but the candle should be shaved or fixed with melted wax so that it does not wobble. Finally, if it is to stand on a precious plate, tray or piece of mirror glass for example, then a small piece of tacky substance will hold it in place. Having overcome the mechanical difficulties, the candle, or candles, is ready to be accompanied by plant material, baubles or simple wood-shaving curls. Remember not to overcrowd the candle, because it would be a shame for it to disappear as it burns. Most important of all, absolutely nothing must be in the path of the flame, because so much of the accompanying material is likely to be inflammable.

As it is likely to command the centre of attention, the base of the decoration has to receive attention to detail. Reflective materials, whether they are paper-backed foil or sprayed with metallic paper, create a satisfactory effect. An attractive decoration can be made with natural wood shavings and wooden beads. No table decoration for an evening Christmas feast would be complete without candles. How splendid it would be to imitate the tables of our forefathers, piled high with food and decoration and a host of candles to light the entire room on their own.

A traditional part of the English table is the Christmas cracker or bon-bon, invented by Tom Smith in 1840. This form of decorative parcel wrapping is an elaborate cylinder, which has a choke on either end to retain a tiny gift. Nearing the end of the meal, these are pulled apart with one's neighbour. To the sounds of the cracks as the strip of saltpetre explodes, the person lucky enough to receive the centre part gains the present within. These crackers can transform a simple table into one of sparkling splendour. Piled onto the table there is often little space left for further decoration, but an arrangement of paper flowers can be made with the materials remaining from the crackers. Not only does this enhance the table with the crackers, but ensures that the table is not left bare when all the crackers have been pulled.

Paper ships—see page 104.

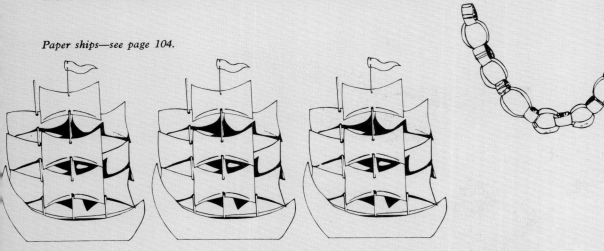

Christmas

There is another way of decorating the table, apart from the candles or the flowers, and that is to use foil for paper sculpture. A procession down the centre, of angels, kings, cockerels or the three ships, lends itself to this form of decoration. Aluminium foil is an excellent material to use as it can be crumpled and squeezed into any shape, either over a mould or on its own. The more adventurous could try a reindeer pulling a sleigh, all made with aluminium foil. It is an easy material to obtain as it may already have its place in the kitchen store cupboard.

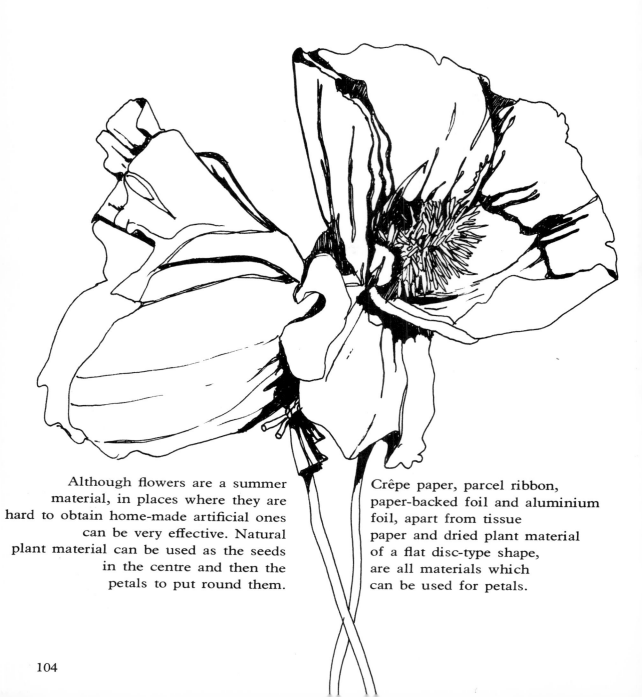

Although flowers are a summer material, in places where they are hard to obtain home-made artificial ones can be very effective. Natural plant material can be used as the seeds in the centre and then the petals to put round them.

Crêpe paper, parcel ribbon, paper-backed foil and aluminium foil, apart from tissue paper and dried plant material of a flat disc-type shape, are all materials which can be used for petals.

A fir-cone garland.

Using the fir-cones as a base, scales from larger fir-cones can be glued between the scales of the smaller ones. These flowers can dominate a swag which can be made entirely with different types of fir-cones. Accompanied by tiny bows of shiny red ribbon, which provides a suggestion of colour, the whole design is sprayed with clear varnish (see colour illustration). Garlands, or in fact streamers, made with paper roses and small pieces of greenery can decorate many places.

The roses are made by cutting twelve petal shapes and moulding them to produce a cup in the centre with the top edges curled over. The first petal should be rolled round the stem, then each consecutive one added, by binding with a continuous piece of wire. Entwine the banisters, make an arch over a doorway or window, or decorate along the mantelpiece and descend on either end, or along a book shelf; these are a few suggestions for their use. This particular garland is made with a little ribbon added to lighten the final effect. The greenery could be sprayed, but it is advisable to test a piece first because if it tends to disappear into the branches it may be a wasted and costly procedure.

A spray or wreath of flowers attached to the front door is a charming way to welcome Christmas visitors. It is quite natural to put an arrangement of artificial flowers in a container on a table or shelf, but the space may be occupied by cards, so try removing a picture temporarily and putting flowers in its place. Parcel ribbon can be used to accompany the paper roses in a stoneware ceramic wall vase. Poppy seeds are used for the centres of one type, with petals made by simply looping parcel ribbon and binding the ends together under the poppy seedhead. Fir-cone rosettes are the third variety which are simply a bow rosette with a fir-cone attached to the centre.

It would seem that every corner has been suggested for decoration by now, although many people prefer to have none of their decorations standing around but to hang them pendulously at vantage points, or to drape the walls. It is always a friendly sight to see the interior of a home decorated for Christmas.

Just as the star hung over the stable at Bethlehem, a star hanging in a window can be symbolic of the Christmas message. The star can be made of simple straw material or be a fantasia type made with parcel ribbon or foil. Ribbon can be used for quilling and circles can be built up and stapled together. For a more sparkling type of star symbol, paper-backed foil used double can be folded in half again into a cone type shape. Then various cuts should be made on either side, taking care to do several small ones rather than large ones, which may result in collapse. Open out the paper to form a paper doily in foil. Children will no doubt be very willing to help with this kind of decoration.

Chains of various kinds are always entertaining to make. The traditional paper chain made with strips of paper links is still an old favourite. All types of paper, coloured foil, or tissue are effective as well as parcel ribbon, and metallic string. One type of streamer which is always fascinating is the concertina variety. On close inspection, a simple version is not so impossible to make. First cut a template with several slits in it, then cut more, adding to them according to length of streamer required. Join two together by stapling on either side. Then add the third one by stapling it to the second one in the centre only. Continue joining each piece in alternate positions and the shape will soon emerge.

Making Christmas decorations can be a family happening in which everyone can be involved. A walk through the wood or countryside will produce a wealth of useful treasures, which can be combined with inexpensive materials. The reward is much greater if satisfying results have been obtained from such contributions. Try not to make the decorations so sophisticated that the children's efforts are hidden; they will be very proud of their decorations alongside the others, and find them a great outlet for Christmas excitement.

Much enjoyment can be gained from making decorations. So whilst the special favourites are bound to be carefully kept from year to year, don't keep everything so that all the planning, gathering and assembling is barred from inclusion in future Christmases.

¡BUENAS FIESTAS
DE NAVIDAD!

Establ. Benziger & Co. S. A Dép 4188 Einsiedeln, Suiz. S

Joyeux Noël!

Buon Natale

Papa

Cards

Each year, hundreds of thousands of people all over the world send and receive Christmas cards. But have you ever wondered when and where the first card was produced? You might think that exchanging cards at Christmas is a very ancient custom—in fact it is barely 100 years old.

The idea of exchanging illustrated greetings and presents is, however, ancient. The Egyptians gave each other symbolic gifts such as inscribed scarabs to celebrate the New Year, while the Romans exchanged golden laurels or strerae (sometimes made of olive branches). Lamps bearing the inscription 'May the New Year by happy and lucky for you' were also given.

In Europe in the 15th century prints were produced by wood engravers that were in effect the prototype of the modern Christmas card. These were inscribed with various legends generally wishing a Happy New Year. Printed greetings, especially from merchants, were commonplace in the 18th and early 19th century, but they were not true Christmas cards.

The first commercial Christmas card as such was produced in Britain in 1843 by Henry Cole, founder of the Victoria and Albert Museum, London. Cole had a design by J. C. Horsley, R.A., lithographed and offered for sale at Felix Summerley's Treasure House in Bond Street, a firm in which he had a financial interest. The hand-coloured print was inscribed with the words 'A Merry Christmas and a Happy New Year to You'. It was horizontally rectangular in shape, printed on stout cardboard by lithography. The design was divided into three parts by rustic poles and vines. The centre part showed a family engaging in the festivities of Christmas, while the two side panels showed scenes of Christmas charity. Space was left at the top to record the name of the recipient and at the bottom to record the name of the sender. The experiment was a failure and Cole did not repeat his venture. Another card, strongly inspired by the Cole experiment, was published by W. M. Egley in 1848. In the United States a similar experiment was made with a card which also drew its inspiration from the Cole/Horsley

card. It was published by R. H. Pease of Albany, New York.

The idea of the Christmas card probably originated in the monastic houses of Britain, where it was the practice to make and exchange ornamented texts and pictures at the more important festivals. Amateur painters during the latter half of the 18th century followed this by drawing or painting sketches which they enclosed in folders and gave as presents. The advent of the penny post in 1840 made possible the sending of cards, but it was not until the 1860's that the Christmas card as we know it came into being. Stationers began selling sheets of writing paper decorated with hand-coloured lithographs of holly sprigs, hampers etc. These were superseded by cards the size of visiting cards with the simple greeting 'A Merry Christmas' set within an embossed border. Sold at 1d. each, they became very popular.

Throughout the Victorian period most of the cards tended to be New Year cards rather than Christmas cards—those with puritanical traditions found it hard to associate any kind of merriment with Christmas or a religious festival. From 1860 onwards the demand for Christmas cards grew steadily. The size of the card was increased and the designs became more elaborate; turkeys, fireside scenes, plum puddings, etc., being popular themes. About this time, too, there appeared an entirely different type of card—well, new to Christmas. In fact it was the earlier Valentine card in a new Christmas guise. Folded sheets of white paper were ornamented with borders of overlapping lace that lifted to form a raised framework for a central picture. The golden gates that once

The first Christmas card designed by J. C. Horsley for Henry Cole. Published in 1843 it was sold at Felix Summerley's Treasure House in Bond Street, London.

opened to display hearts aflame on the altar of love now disclosed 'The Compliments of the Season' or 'A Happy New Year to You'.

In the United States sentiment cards had been exchanged from about 1830 to the 1860s. One of the first commercial Christmas cards in the U.S. seems to have been adapted from one of these. Perhaps the real founder of the American Christmas card can be said to be Louis Prang of Boston. He printed a wide variety of album cards and visiting cards, and in 1875 issued seasonal greeting cards which were an immediate success.

The children's cards of 1870 are very interesting in that they show a marked difference between the Christmas customs of that time compared with those of the present day. Present-giving was mainly associated with the New Year. One popular card depicted a child sitting up in bed surrounded by toys; beneath the picture were the words 'New Year, New Joys, New Books, New Toys.' Another

Die besten Weihnachtsgrüsse

ХРИСТОС СЕ РОДИ.

card, showing a row of stockings hung on a tree, had the following rhyme:

> *Hang stockings high,*
> *Christmas is nigh.*
> *And birds will surely find them,*
> *And when they go,*
> *They will, I know,*
> *Leave many gifts behind them.*

May this and c FU years be

E. Hildesheimer & Co.

Blwydyn Newydd
da i chwi

Joyeux Noël

West Cliff Hotel
West cliff on Sea

much love & all good wishes
from Odette M.D.

The fashion of mounting greeting cards in albums completely changed the style of the Christmas card. No longer was it regarded solely as a carrier of good wishes, but as a new picture to be added to the collection. Verses were transferred to the back and the picture became the all-important feature. Popular scenes of this period were the traditional wintry subjects as well as more unusual subjects such as children playing by the sea, or boats moored beneath weeping willows.

The advent of chromo-lithography enabled new heights to be reached in the production of cards and many fine studies of flowers and butterflies, etc., were produced.

ompliments
of the Season.
sons come and go—
Christmas now is here,
n in one short week,
ollows the New Year
iness be yours kind f———
om the New Year to its end.

...er & Co.   ...right.

Christmas Greetings

Hearty Christmas Greeting

Accept this Wish, my
much-loved friend, from me,
That at this festive season,
happy you may be.

By 1880 the popularity of Christmas cards was such that manufacturers were able to offer more attractive rewards to artists engaged on designs, and thus provide an incentive to raise the artistic standards of the cards. In Britain, prizes of several hundred pounds were offered for original designs, and many prominent artists of the time had their work reproduced on Christmas cards.

1880 was also the year in which the now familiar 'Post early for Christmas' pleas were issued to the public by the Postmaster-General. Since then, cards have progressed by leaps and bounds until the present day when we see the Christmas card not only being produced by manufacturers for profit, but by charities while the Post Offices of many countries of the world have issued special stamps, aerogrammes and seals. The first Christmas postal seal in fact originated in Denmark in 1904. They were designed by Einar Holbøll for the National Tuberculosis Association. By the mid-20th century over $25,000,000 was being raised annually by this means.

As Christmas changes, so do Christmas cards, but the sentiment they record remains the same:
'Peace and goodwill to all men'

Saints

The two words 'Santa Claus' conjure up for us the whole spirit of Christmas. We picture him, a jolly old gentleman with his white whiskers and his rosy cheeks, dressed in his gay, fur-trimmed coat and hood and driving his reindeer team through the skies with merry cracks of his whip.

Saint Nicholas

But when we stop to enquire what lies behind this happy picture, we find some very curious things. To begin with, Saint Nicholas—that was his name to start with—is about the most overworked saint who ever existed. He is the national saint of Russia and Greece, and the patron saint of many European cities; and churches named after him can be numbered in thousands—there are more than 400 in Great Britain alone. If one started to list all the groups of people who look on him as their patron saint, it would seem endless. One encyclopaedia gives the following: judges, murderers, pawnbrokers, thieves, merchants, paupers, scholars and sailors; others add bakers, travellers, maidens and children—poor children especially. He is known as the friend and protector of all those in trouble.

The legends about him are legion. Sailors own him as their particular saint because he is said often to have appeared to them during violent storms and saved their lives. Sick children have been brought back to health through his influence. Perhaps the most famous story of all tells how he helped three unfortunate young sisters who all had suitors, but were unable to marry because their father, a poor nobleman, could not raise the money for their dowries, without which marriage was impossible in those days. Saint Nicholas, who was then Bishop of Myra, his home town on the coast of what is now Turkey, came to hear of their plight; but, being a shy man, he did not like to give them money directly, so found a way to do it anonymously. One version of the story says that for three nights running he threw purses filled with gold in at the window of the girls' home; another version says that he climbed on the roof and threw the purses down the chimney so that they landed in the stockings which the girls had hung up by the fire to dry. Is this perhaps the origin of the custom of the Christmas stocking?

One thing is certain, three purses of gold did come into the story somewhere. Statues of the bishop often show him holding three balls to symbolise them; and there is not much doubt that that is the origin of the three balls which are the symbol of the pawnbroker, though these gentlemen are not always known for their generosity, as the saint was.

But how much do we actually know about Saint Nicholas himself? Not very much. We do not even know the date of his birth; but, strangely enough, we do know the date of his death. It was December 6, in either A.D. 345 or 352; that date has become sacred to the celebrating of Christmas in many European countries, Holland in particular.

We should not have known very much more than that if he had been left to lie quietly in his grave. But in those days the bodies of holy men were of very great value, not only spiritually but commercially; and when some merchant seamen from the port of Bari in south-eastern Italy heard a rumour that the Venetians were coming to carry off the saint's body they determined to forestall them. On May 9, 1087, they made a raid on Myra, seized the saint's remains and carried them back home to Bari, where they are to this day in the beautiful Basilica of Saint Nicholas, which was built to house them. There the faithful through the centuries have visited them and have sometimes experienced miracles. They have prayed to the saint, who was known to have had such a care for all who are poor and needy, whether in mind or body.

But the changes were not over yet for this hard-worked saint. During his lifetime he was said to have been tall and thin and stately; but the Dutch settlers who emigrated to America took their beloved saint with them—Sinter Klass, as they called him, or Santa Claus, as it became in the United States; and he began to take on a

St. Nicholas

Greek Icon of St. Nicholas

Saint Wenceslas

very different appearance. Washington Irving, in his book *Knickerbocker's History of New York* (1809), in which he claimed the saint as the guardian of New York City, created a new image of him, looking very much like a typical Dutch settler. Probably that is where the jolly red face and the whiskers came in. When Clement C. Moore in 1822 wrote his poem "Twas the night before Christmas', he described the Santa Claus we have today, with his eight tiny reindeer flying over the rooftops in his joyous, gift-laden ride.

And that is how the serious, stately saint of the 4th century became the homely, well-loved figure whom every child rejoices to meet in the shops at Christmas, and whom many of them half expect to come down the chimney at night to fill the stockings which they have hopefully hung ready for him, a hope which is rarely disappointed.

The second saint associated with Christmas is a very surprising one. If you were to go to Czechoslovakia and visit Prague, its capital city, you would find in its main square a statue of its patron saint, and the square itself is called after him. There he stands, the figure of quite a young man; and round the base of his statue is carved the prayer: 'Saint Wenceslas, suffer not us nor our children to perish.' For this young saint is none other than the hero of one of our favourite Christmas carols, 'good king Wenceslas'.

We always picture him as a kindly old gentleman in royal robes and with a long white beard, plodding through the snow, while his page treads in his footsteps, carrying the basket of provisions, the meat and wine which they are taking to the poor peasant whom the king has seen from his palace window. But this picture could not be farther from the truth. Wenceslas lived in violent times, and he met a cruel death at the age of only 22. But the way he lived during those few short years has ensured that the world has never forgotten him.

He was born in the early years of the 10th century A.D., 600 years or so after Saint Nicholas, into a troubled age. Christianity was competing for the minds of men. The battle was being fought even in Wenceslas' own family, for his grandfather, King Borivoj of Bohemia (today part of Czechoslovakia), and his grandmother Ludmilla were both Christians, as was their son Wratislav; and they hoped that their two grandsons, Wenceslas and Boleslav, would be the same, and make their land a Christian nation. But Wratislav had married a princess called Drahomira, who belonged to one of the pagan tribes which surrounded Bohemia; and though she was a nominal Christian, her mental processes were still pagan.

This came out when King Wratislav died, and Wenceslas, who was only 12 and so too young to succeed to the throne, was put in charge of his grandmother Ludmilla, while Queen Drahomira ruled as regent. The nobles in her court, many of whom were pagans, did not approve of this arrangement, and told the queen that if the young prince was allowed to stay with his grandmother she would turn him into a monk, who would not be fit to rule. Drahomira agreed with them and banished the queen mother to a distant castle. Not content with that, she sent men to strangle the old lady as she was praying in the castle chapel. Those were indeed violent times.

They must have been difficult and dangerous days for young Prince Wenceslas, with his mother and her nobles putting pressure on him to live in the pagan way. But he was a fighter, and learnt to read and write, an unusual accomplishment in those days even for nobles and kings, so that he could read the Bible for himself and learn more about his faith. He also had Christian priests smuggled into the palace at night to teach him more.

He was physically courageous too, as was shown when the Duke of Bavaria attacked Bohemia. Though Wenceslas was only 13 or 14, he put himself at the head of his troops, and beat off the invaders. The people rallied to him, and by the time he was about 18 he felt strong enough to take over the country and rule as a Christian king. One of his first acts was to banish his mother from court, as she had banished his grandmother. "There is to be no more killing," he said. Later he allowed her to return to court, but she had no more power in the land.

Wenceslas was a good king. Though he sternly upheld law and order, he cared for his people, saw that the chldren were well educated and that the army was properly trained and equipped. It is said that he bought people about to be sold as slaves in order to set them free. And he cut down as much as possible the number of death sentences for offenders. The story of how he and his page Podiven helped the poor peasant at Christmas is typical of him. He was full of courage, and once, when he was 21, he engaged in single combat with the leader of an invading tribe. He defeated him and the invaders were obliged to depart. He was wise too, and when the King of Saxony, Henry the Fowler, attacked him with a force too large for his own army to take on, he made a treaty with him and agreed to pay him tribute, while at the same time making friends with him and working to turn him from an enemy into an ally.

But then, after only two years of Wenceslas' wise reign, violence broke out again. The pagan nobles did not like the king's way of ruling, and they conspired with his brother Boleslav, who was bitterly jealous of him and angry at what he had done to their mother. They decided to kill the king. Boleslav invited him to the dedication of a chapel in his own castle, and there, when he was at service, Boleslav had the doors locked and himself aimed the first blow at his brother. The faithful page Podiven defended his master and killed one of the murderers, for which he was later hanged; but Wenceslas fell under their daggers, and Boleslav took over the

throne.

But he found that he too was obliged to pay tribute to Henry the Fowler, and to adopt many of his dead brother's wise measures. The people of Bohemia never forgot their good king Wenceslas. His statue still stands in Wenceslas Square, and we remember him every Christmas when we sing his well-loved carol.

Saint Francis

The third saint of Christmas came some 200 years later—Saint Francis of Assisi. But what has he to do with Christmas, you may ask? It is not generally known that it was he who was responsible for that ever more popular feature of the season—the Christmas crib. It is everywhere nowadays at Christmas, from the simple group of figures in the home and the rather more elaborate ones in churches and shop windows to the magnificent *presepio*, such as I saw in a Catholic church in Nairobi, Kenya. It took up the whole of one wall inside a darkened building, and showed a street of little houses—Bethlehem at night, with lights twinkling in many of the windows. A Christmas carol was being softly played; and, as we watched, morning came, the sky lightened, the little lights in the houses went out one by one, and there in the foreground was the holy family, the ox and ass, sheep and camels, shepherds and wise men, in all their familiar glory.

But how did Saint Francis come to be the initiator of this beautiful visual aid to the keeping of Christmas? It was all part of his longing to make the great truths of the spirit real to the ordinary person. Francis was one of the most real people that ever lived. Everything and everybody was real to him, and he loved them all. He loved people, from the great Pope in his palace—he knew two of them—to the beggars in the streets, the robbers in the mountains, and especially the wretched lepers, who had to live away from all other people for fear of infection. Francis loved all creatures too. He loved the birds; most people know the story of how he preached to them and how they perched all round him to hear him, flying away when he dismissed them. He loved the beasts too, even the fierce wolf who terrified the people of Gubbio, and whom he is said to have tamed. He once begged the Emperor to pass a law that all birds and beasts should be given extra food at Christmas, that happy festival which he loved so much, so that they too might have 'joy in the Lord'.

He loved things as well, especially the beautiful clothes which he wore as a young man, and which were made for him from the gorgeous velvets and satins and other costly materials which his father Pietro Bernardone, the rich cloth merchant, sold in his shop. People tended to wear their wealth on their backs in those days, and Bernardone was happy to see his son, the best dressed young man in town, leading all the other young people in music and dancing and

Opposite: *St. Francis with the birds.*

general roistering—it was all good for business, in which he hoped that Francis would join him one day.

But Francis, although he was the gayest young man about town, with his French songs and his viol and lute, began to find that things as such did not satisfy him. He felt that there must be something more real in the world, and he tried all sorts of ways to find it. He even went to war, but it only landed him as a captive in prison, and he came home very weak after a serious illness.

But at last he found that for him real satisfaction was to be found in loving God and doing what He wanted. He found this new way of living so satisfying and demonstrated it so well that other people began to follow him. He longed to make the great truths of the spirit real to them, and one Christmas time he had the idea of showing people just what the birth of Jesus really must have been like, in all its poverty and discomfort. He found exactly the right place for it—a great pile of rocks on a bleak mountain near the village of Greccio. In a cleft of the mountainside there was a cave, and there he decided to rebuild the Nativity scene. He brought up an ox and an ass, and had the figure of a baby carved and laid in the manger between them. News of what he was doing spread all over the countryside, and towards the cave on the steep, desolate mountain a steady stream of men, women and children came by night carrying torches and candles to light their way, till at last they were all massed around the entrance to the cave, and looking in.

'It seemed like midday,' wrote someone who was there, 'during that midnight filled with gladness for man and beast, and the crowds drawing near, so happy to be present for the renewal of the eternal mystery.' Francis himself sang the Gospel story in a voice which was 'strong, sweet and clear,' says the observer. 'Then he preached to the people, most movingly, about the birth of the poor King in little Bethlehem.' And the observer goes on to tell how a man who was watching the figure of the baby in the manger saw it open its eyes as Francis stooped over it.

So when we see a crib at Christmas time we can remember the 'little poor man', as he used to call himself, who was able to make great truths as real to other people as they were to him.

Cooking

Feasting has, over the centuries, always been associated with major celebrations, religious or secular, hence the word Festival. Christmas, perhaps more than any other occasion, is celebrated by communal consumption of foods that have become a traditional part of the festival. All countries have their own special dishes, some of which are described here. There are numerous variations of the menus and recipes but they can be adapted with ease by anyone wanting to introduce an international element to their Christmas fare.

In Finland the baking of special breads has become traditional, some of them are pictured opposite. A number of breads are made from the same dough. A typical recipe would be as follows:

RECIPE
Pulla (Pitko)
Pulla Yeast Coffee Bread

Ingredients: 1 packet active dry yeast; ½ cup warm water; 2 cups milk, scalded and cooled; 1 cup (or less) sugar; 1 teaspoon salt; 7-8 cardamom pods, seeded and crushed *or* 1 teaspoon crushed cardamom; 4 eggs, beaten; 8-9 cups sifted white flour; ½ cup melted butter.
Glaze: 1 beaten egg; ½ cup chopped almonds; ½ cup crushed lump sugar.

Method: Dissolve yeast in warm water, add milk, sugar, salt, eggs, cardamom and 2 cups flour. Beat until dough is smooth and elastic. Add 3 cups flour and beat well; dough should be smooth and glossy. Add melted butter and stir in well. Beat until dough looks glossy. Add remaining flour until a stiff dough forms. Turn onto a lightly floured board and cover. Allow to rest 15 minutes. Knead until smooth. Place in a lightly greased mixing bowl, turn cover and let rise in a warm place until double in size (about 1 hour). Knead lightly and allow to rise until almost doubled in size (30 minutes). Shape as required.

The same dough can be used to make Joulukakut (Fancy Christmas Cake), the round bread composite spirals in the illustration opposite.

Certain dishes seem to have been adapted in many countries as traditional. The turkey, plum pudding, and mince pies are in this class.

In France, the home of good food, a Christmas spread may consist of: Grapefruit Baskets; Poached Fillet of Dover Sole; Roast Turkey, Chestnut Stuffing, Cranberry Sauce, Brussels Sprouts and Golden Potatoes; Christmas Pudding and Brandy Sauce; Mince Pies.

Opposite: *Scandinavian Christmas breads.*

Christmas Pudding

Ingredients (3 puddings)
567 gms (1¼ lb) flour
1.13 kilos (2½ lb) raisins
1.13 kilos (2½ lb) suet
142 gms (5 oz) candied lemon peel
57 gms (2 oz) citron peel
1 large nutmeg
20 eggs
1 teaspoon salt
567 gms (1¼ lb) breadcrumbs
1.13 kilos (2½ lb) currants
567 gms (1¼ lb) white moist sugar
85 gms (3 oz) candied orange peel
14 gms (½ oz) mixed spice
2 lemons—grated rind
1 cup milk
284 ml (½ pint) brandy

Method
Mix all ingredients together in large bowl.
Stand overnight. Place in greased
pudding basins and boil for 7-8 hours.
Boil for 2 hours before serving.

Brandy Sauce

Ingredients
1 litre milk
40 gms (1½ oz) arrowroot
200 gms (7 oz) sugar
½ litre brandy

Method
Combine all ingredients except the
brandy and bring to the boil stirring
continuously. When smooth and
thickened add brandy and serve.

RECIPE
Roast Turkey

Pluck and draw your turkey and singe it. Sew the vent. Leave the skin round the neck. Take 500 gms (17½ oz) roast chestnuts; peel them carefully and put them in a pan, the bottom of which is covered with water, with a knob of butter the size of an egg, a bay leaf and a sprig of thyme; season them with salt and pepper and cook them on a low heat for 10-15 minutes; then mix in 500 gms (17½ oz) of sausage meat, cover the pan and cook the sausage meat, stirring from time to time; pour it all into a terrine and let it cool off slightly. When it is just warm stuff your bird with it, pull down the skin of the neck onto the breast and tie it with a string to keep the stuffing in. Having stuffed your turkey put a thick slice of bacon on the bird's breast. Then serve on a dish and pour its juice over it.

This recipe can also be used for traditional English and American fare.

Poached Fillet of Dover Sole

Ingredients (6 servings): 6×113 gm (4 oz) fillets of Dover sole; ¼ litre white wine; 100 gms cepes (optional garnish); 100 gms truffles (optional garnish); 50 gms (2 oz) butter; 50 gms (2 oz) flour; ¼ litre cream; fish stock; salt and pepper; lemon wedges; parsley.

Method: Neatly fold fillets into a dish and half cover with fish stock and white wine. Poach for 10 minutes. Remove fish from stock. Melt butter in another pan and add flour to make a roux. Make sauce using stock and white wine, and simmer for 5 minutes. Add cream and adjust seasoning. Pour sauce over fish and garnish with parsley and lemon. Add cepes and truffles if available.

In Germany every region and town has its own traditions and variations of recipes, many of which have been handed down in families from one generation to another.

A Christmas menu uses seasonal foodstuffs enriched with as many delicacies as the family can afford. Roast turkey, goose or venison may take pride of place. A Christmas lunch may consist of: Westphalian Ham with Melon; Red Wine Soup; Boiled Trout; Horseradish and melted butter; Thuringian Roast Goose, Red Cabbage, Bread Dumplings with Mushrooms; Nut Pudding; Petit Fours.

Thuringian Roast Goose

Ingredients (4 servings): 1×8 lb goose; 1 tablespoon salt; 1 tablespoon dried marjoram; 2 medium onions, peeled; 1 stalk celery, broken in 3-4 pieces; salt; pepper; 6 cloves; 2 apples, well washed; 1 cup chicken or goose stock; 1 cup orange juice; 2 tablespoons cornflour; $\frac{1}{4}$ cup cold water.

Method: Remove giblets and place them in a saucepan with 1 onion, celery pieces, salt and pepper. Cover with water and simmer for 1-1½ hours. Strain and reserve stock. Meanwhile, wash and dry goose. Sprinkle inside and out with salt. Sprinkle inside with Marjoram. Stick cloves in second onion and place in cavity with apples. Skewer openings together. Place goose on rack in a large roasting pan, breast-side down. Roast in hot oven for 45 minutes, drain fat from pan. Reduce oven temperature and roast until tender, approximately 1 hour. Turn goose breast-side up and cook until golden brown—30 minutes. Remove goose to a warm place. Skim off all remaining fat from pan and add stock and orange juice. Mix cornflour and cold water and add to pan. Cook over medium heat, stirring constantly until gravy is thick. Strain over goose.

In Italy in addition to a roast dish the Christmas meal may include a large number of pasta dishes including ravioli, cappelletti, Tagliatelle (fettuccine) and Lasagne. The meal, such as the one illustrated, starts with an antipasto, such as chopped ham salad, which is followed by the pastas. The main dish may be Tacchino Arrosto—roast turkey. Sweets such as those made from chestnuts are popular.

Left: *Thuringian roast Goose and boiled trout.*
Right: *Italian pasta dishes.*

Boiled Trout

Ingredients (4 servings)
4×170 gm (6 oz) trout
227 gms (½ lb) carrots
6 button onions
2 sticks celery
Vinegar
Bayleaf
Peppercorns

Method
Do not wash the fish, but remove the insides only. Remove the fins, taking care not to take away the slime on the outside the fish. Place fish in vinegar and allow t turn blue. Poach fish in water and 71 ml gill) of vinegar, slices of fluted carrot, crescents of celery, rings of button onion peppercorns, bayleaf and parsley for 5 minutes, after bringing to the boil. Serve with grated horseradish to which a little lemon juice has been added and melted butter.

Bread Dumplings with Mushrooms

Ingredients (4 servings)
14 oz loaf, day old French bread
1 cup milk
2 eggs, beaten
1 tablespoon salt
black pepper
4 oz butter
cup finely chopped onions
1 lb fresh mushrooms, sliced
1 tablespoon chopped parsley
6 pints salted water.

Method
Cut bread in very thin slices and soak in warm milk. Add eggs and salt and allow stand for 30 minutes. Saute finely chopped onions in butter until tender, season with salt and black pepper. Add sliced mushrooms and parsley and cook gently for 3 minutes. Remove from heat and add to bread mixture. Blend to an even consistency. In a large saucepan bring salted water to the boil, reduce to a simmer. Shape dumplings with wet hand to size of a large egg (if mixture is too soft add some dry breadcrumbs). Drop dumplings into simmering water and simmer 10-15 minutes. Remove from pan and serve in an earthenware dish with a little browned butter.

Nut Pudding

Ingredients
75 gms (2½ oz) sugar
75 gms (2½ oz) butter
3 eggs, separated
60 gms (2 oz) hazelnuts, grated
40 gms (1½ oz) cornstarch
sachet of vanilla flavoured sugar
3 dessertspoons of biscuit crumbs.

Method
Beat the butter and 2 dessertspoons sugar until light. Add egg yolks and beat. Whisk the egg whites until stiff and then fold in the remaining sugar. With a metal spoon fold this into the butter mixture, and then fold in most of the hazelnuts, the biscuit crumbs, cornstarch and vanilla sugar. Pour this into a well greased dish that has been sprinkled with the remaining nuts ensuring that the dish is not more than three quarters full. Put a lid on the dish and place in a saucepan of simmering water that does not cover more than half the dish. Cook slowly for about 35 minutes or until set.

Roast Saddle of Venison

Ingredients (4 servings)
1½ kilos (3 lbs) saddle of venison
  pears
200 gms (7 oz) cranberries
250 ml (scant ½ pt) red wine
  oranges
200 gms (7 oz) button onions
½ kilo (1 lb) butter
½ kilo (1 lb) margarine
50 gms (2 oz) juniper berries
125 ml (scant ¼ pt) sour cream
200 gms (7 oz) speck (or bacon fat)
200 gms (7 oz) celery
100 gms (3½ oz) leeks

Method
Stud venison with square strips of speck. Before cooking marinate for 3 days with red wine, juniper berries, carrots, a few drops of oil, celery, leeks and onions. Remove from marinade, cover with fresh sliced speck and roast in a moderate oven for 40 minutes. This will result in the meat being rare and pink (see illustration). Add another 40 minutes at a lower heat. If you prefer the meat well done add another 40 minutes at a lower heat. When cooked lift the meat out of the tin and leave to rest. Put the vegetables from the marinade in the roasting tin and brown on the top of the cooker. Skim the fat from the roasting tin, add the marinade to the vegetables and continue cooking until reduced to a sauce. Finish with sour cream and adjust seasoning.

Dutch Christmas fare including Roast saddle of Venison, Christmas wreath and Sinterklaas Initials.

A feature of Dutch Christmas fare is the Christmas Wreath and Sinterklaas Initials—see illustration. The main meal generally takes place in the evening, when families gather around their candle-lit tables set with accents of red, green and white. Roast hare, goose and venison have been traditional favourites, but the turkey is fast becoming the most popular. The Christmas meal illustrated consists of: Dutch Cheese Salad; Roast Saddle of Venison, Brussels Sprouts, Braised Chestnuts, Roast Potatoes, Butter Onions and Carrots; Christmas Wreath; Sinterklaas Initials.

Sinterklaas Initials & Christmas Wreath

Ingredients: ½ cup unsalted butter; 1 cup sifted flour; ¼ cup ice water; pinch of salt; 113 gms (¼ lb) blanched almonds; ½ cup sugar; 1 egg; pinch of salt.

Method: Make puff paste dough. While it chills, prepare the almond paste. Grind the blanched almonds and mix with the sugar, beaten egg, grated peel and salt. Grind this mixture once more. On a floured board, roll it into a number of sausages about 1″ in diameter. Wrap in waxpaper and chill. After final chilling period roll out the dough into a strip 3½″ wide and ⅛″ thick. Place sausages end to end along centre, fold dough over it and seal top and ends with water.

Shape into required initial and place, seam down, on a floured cookie sheet. Brush with beaten egg diluted with water. Bake 30-35 minutes in 425° oven. Cool on rack. The Christmas Wreath uses the same ingredients as Sinterklaas Initials. After shaping it is baked as before. When cool, spread with confectioners' icing and decorate lavishly with red and green glacéed cherries and 'leaves' cut from candied citron.

Apart from the roast dish which has changed over the years due to changing fashion, the Christmas pudding which has been made for centuries has remained the main Christmas traditional dish in Britain. A typical 18th century recipe is as follows:

RECIPE
Christmas Pudding of King George I
Ingredients: 1½ lbs finely shredded suet; 1 lb eggs, weighed in their shells; 1 lb each dried plums, stoned and halved; mixed peel, cut in long strips; small raisins; sultanas; currants; sifted flour; sugar; brown crumbs; 1 heaped teaspoon mixed spice; ½ nutmeg, grated; 2 teaspoons salt; ½ pint new milk; Juice 1 lemon; Large wineglass brandy.

Method: Mix dry ingredients and moisten with eggs, beaten to a froth. Add the milk, lemon juice and brandy. Stand for at least 12 hours in a cool place then turn into buttered moulds. Boil for 8 hours, then for 2 hours before serving. Makes 3×3 lb puddings.

Another recipe
Christmas Pudding with Carrots and Old Ale
Ingredients: 14 oz beef suet, grated; 14 oz currants; 8 oz mixed peel; 8 oz stoned raisins; 10 oz sultanas; 1 oz ground almonds; 7 oz flour; pinch salt; ⅛ oz baking powder; 7 oz breadcrumbs; ⅛ teaspoon ground nutmeg; ¼ teaspoon ground cinnamon; ⅛ teaspoon mixed spice; 4 oz carrots; 8 oz Demerara sugar; Rind and Juice of ½ lemon; 3 eggs; 1 gill old ale; Silver pudding favours.

Method: Place all dry ingredients and fruit in a large mixing bowl, cover and leave overnight. Next day, stir in ale and strained lemon juice with your hand until evenly mixed. Beat eggs in a basin and add to mixture, stirring with your hand. Use 2 more eggs if required, or a little more ale. Beat well and add favours. Grease basins and fill to within 1″ of top to allow room for rising. Cover with buttered paper and tie securely; tie up with pudding cloths and steam for 7 hours. Store in a dry, airy cupboard until required then steam for 2 hours before serving. Makes two large puddings.

Whatever the dish—whether rich or poor—it is the sentiment that is and has always been important, a family celebration honouring the birth of Christ with the harvest of the earth.

Dutch Cheese Salad

Ingredients (4 servings)
250 gms (8¾ oz) garlic sausage
250 gms (8¾ oz) Edam cheese
100 gms (3½ oz) onion
1 clove garlic
125 ml (scant ¼ pint) olive oil
125 ml (scant ¼ pint) wine vinegar
200 gms Dutch pickled cucumber
Lemon
Parsley
2 hard boiled eggs.

Method
Rub bowl with crushed garlic. Cut the garlic sausage, onion, cheese and cucumber into fine strips. Season with olive oil, wine vinegar, salt and pepper and lemon. Pile into prepared bowl and garnish with hard boiled eggs and parsley

Stories
for
Christmas

Hole in the Sock

The noise was brutal in the discotheque at the Mena Hotel. Although we were in a Moslem country, they had decorated the bar and the bandstand with silver bells and plastic stars, with a brightly painted sign from the management wishing all and sundry a merry Christmas. Paper hats out of crackers bobbed up and down amid the fez, the flowing Arab head-scarves, glittering Western hair-does, and long-haired males.

The bar was busy dispensing Christmas cheer and now the pop group, who obviously came from the West, and who called themselves 'The Shepherds', were winding up with their own peculiar version of a familiar carol. To me the whole atmosphere was depressing. "Come on," I said, grabbing my friend Rupa by the arm. "Let's for goodness' sake get out of here."

Outside, the air was cold, the stars were bright, and in the moonlight the great pyramids looked down, serene and dispassionate, on the latest antics of that busy little animal called man. "Let's go up to our room, light a candle, and sing Christmas carols," I said. We were both of us Hindus, but we had been brought up in Mission school, and we knew the old carols by heart. "Why not?" said Rupa. "Tomorrow we'll have fun lying in the sun, taking photos and riding ponies round the pyramids. But tonight let's be cosy and Christmassy and talk about home. I even bought you a present in Bombay." We had a three-day stop-over in Cairo.

It was by the elevators that Modi, the Air Asia Personnel Supervisor, caught us. "Hello, girls," he said, with that toothy smile that he put on when he wanted something out of you. "Merry Christmas!" We didn't respond, waiting for the next bit. It came all right. "Glad I've found you," he said. "I've a nice little Christmas surprise for one of you lucky people." "Come on," I said. "Out with it! I know! Someone's dropped out of the crew on the London flight, and you're looking for a replacement. Right?" "How did you guess? I can't order you to go, but one of you will just have to volunteer. The pick-up bus leaves in half an hour."

"Oh," said Rupa, "I was looking forward to that pony. What do we do? Toss for it?" "Don't bother," I said. "I'll do it. You've done me some good turns in your day." "Do you really mean it? You're an angel." "Why not? Christmas spirit and all that. I've friends in London. English turkey and plum pudding have their charms." I didn't tell her another reason. One of the boys in that pop group looked quite nice. He had mentioned earlier in the evening as we just happened to chat that this was their last show in Egypt. They were on the Air Asia night flight to London. Might be fun. Who knows? His name was Mike. There was another reason deeper still, so deep that I did not even tell it to myself. I just had a strange urge, a hunch, whatever you call it, that this Christmas was going to be different. If only something worthwhile might happen for once. Something new.

There was barely time to slip on a sari, paint my finger-nails and to apply to my forehead the small coloured circle, the tikka, that all Air Asia hostesses wear on the job. It was a mad rush, followed of course, as usual, by long waits, calls around Cairo, to collect other members of the crew, and then the discovery that the plane was coming in late from Bombay, and that we would not be out of Cairo till well after midnight. At the airport the lounges and the main departure hall were crowded with travellers, jostling, queue-jumping, arguing, protesting or else slumped exhausted on benches, in that resigned stupor that air travel induces.

All the planes seemed to be late, all departures delayed. Most connections disrupted. The steady drone of the loudspeaker kept up a stream of announcements and apologies all adding up to uncertainty and frustration. It was Christmas Eve, and everybody was wanting to get home or get somewhere in double-quick time. As I hurried through the main lounge I noticed a young Arab woman, dressed in traditional blue with white veil and head-dress. She was lying uncomfortably on a bench, her head propped on a bundle, while her husband nearby was queuing anxiously for a possible last-minute no-show seat on our flight. Every now and then he looked back at his wife with a wan, loving smile. She returned it bravely. She was bundled up with rugs and shawls and looked deathly ill. I gave her a quick smile and hoped they'd be in luck tonight. They needed it.

I walked on into the personnel lounge where things were more quiet and orderly. Unconsciously, we picked up the rhythm of a routine departure. Then action stations.

The majority of the passengers were already on board. Some of them had made connections all the way from Australia. They were tired and numb and a few were bad-tempered, full of questions and complaints from the word 'go'. It's always a bit tough to be held personally to blame for every mishap or misadventure on all the air-lines from Perth to London. But that's part of the game. What are hostesses for? Anyway there wasn't too much time to bother about that, amid all the turmoil of pre-take-off.

The new passengers on board must be welcomed with a smile. That insipid pre-take-off music has been switched on. It's supposed to soothe nervous stomachs. I see 'The Shepherds' have made it all right. They are safe on board, their instruments reverently stowed away in our already too-cramped quarters. But they're here, and it looks as if they're in my section. That's good. It may be fun later on. Meanwhile there's no time to think of anything except the job, the take-off.

I've been an air-hostess now for nearly five years, but I've never lost the thrill, the drama of the take-off, especially at night. Suddenly everything becomes a vast stage. Curtain up. Lights, sound, action. And there am I somehow centre stage. Actually, of course, it's only the smallest bit-part that I'm playing, but believe me there are moments when I feel like the leading lady. "Please fasten your seat-belts, extinguish your cigarettes, make sure your seats are in the upright position. Welcome on board Air-Asia flight so-and-so, etc. etc." Then all over again in different languages. Then follows the mime bit; we demonstrate the safety jackets, how you put them on. You make it all very matter-of-fact, as an actress may 'throw away' important lines. Only a few inexperienced passengers take much notice. Wait one day until it actually happens, and we all find ourselves in the sea, blowing up those life jackets, fumbling for that whistle so thoughtfully provided. It all goes so smoothly a thousand times. But you never quite forget, especially in days of bombs and hijacking, that the act could

suddenly turn into real life, and you could be the leading lady all
right, with a vengeance.

    This time it was all just another piece of cake. The place was
full, the passengers tired and out-of-sorts, but they were mostly too
relieved to be air-borne at last to want to make much fuss. The
Shepherds soon fell asleep, except for the boy Mike who had taken
my fancy. He had asked for his guitar and was half out in the aisle
strumming and worrying away at a new song. Just behind, at the
very rear of the plane, the young Palestinian couple were hunched
in the back seat. I gave them one of my very special hostess smiles
and told them how glad I was that they had made the plane. The
husband told me that they had come thumbing their way to Amman
and then by plane to Cairo, where they had been delayed at the
airport two or three days, desperately trying to get seats on a flight to
London. I asked him why they were travelling, and he said
something about their village being deliberately burned and destroyed. Their home was gone, his wife urgently needed medical
attention. Friends in England had invited them to stay, so they had
sold everything, the family jewels and all, and decided to go; and

could his wife have a cup of coffee or soup, and perhaps another blanket? It was obvious that she was pregnant. Her voluminous robes must have concealed the fact earlier or she would never have been allowed on the plane.

After the drinks and the meal, we dimmed the cabin lights and people settled down to sleep; all except my friend Mike, who seemed to have a song on the brain, a funny little lyric struggling to be born. "Save me from myself. Save me from myself.

> I don't know what to do,
> I can't discover who
> I am."

One of the drowsier passengers across the aisle was getting fed up. "If you can't save yourself, at least you can save us. Whoever you are I wish you'd pipe down." I took the chance to go along and strike up a conversation. He was a nice boy really, utterly absorbed in what he was doing. He talked about his family in Wales. They'd all be in chapel together Christmas morning. That's where he'd learnt his music. When he left home, and joined the group and started to travel, the family had cut him off and would have nothing more to do with him. To them a pop group meant rootless living, a lack of morals, with dope thrown in, and above all disgrace in the eyes of the godly chapelites, among whom he had been brought up. But when your whole being thirsted for one thing, to compose and sing songs, to express what you were feeling in words and music, what else could you do? "Join a nice Welsh male voice choir," he said, "and sing at Aberystwyth and Cwm Rhondda, 'Guide me, O thou great Redeemer' till the cows come home? Not likely!" "I bet you miss it all at Christmas all the same," I said. "Anyway, some of those old hymns sound a bit more cheerful than what you seem to be churning out." I couldn't resist teasing him a little. Mike rose to the bait. "I got the idea of this one," he said, "from an old bloke I happened to meet outside a mosque in Cairo. Some sort of a holy man or something, a proper guru. I go out of my way talking to odd types like that. I suppose it's the chapel in me coming out. He was a bit of a screwball, but quite human. Could listen as well as talk. I found myself giving him some edited selections from the story of my life. He seemed interested. I had barely got to some of the seamier details when he interrupted and said, 'It seems to me, brother, what you need is saving from yourself.' I thanked him next day. I think he was hoping he'd made some kind of a convert, but I told him he'd done something much better than that; he'd given me an idea for a song. 'Save me from myself.' Can't you see it big in the charts?" I hadn't the heart to tell him I thought it a certain flop, so I just said, "Well, good luck with it, but I'd keep it down if you can. You're annoying the passengers."

"I'll say he is," said an American lady across the gangway.

"I've flown in 34 different planes in my trip round the world and this is the worst flight yet. Can't you find me another seat, stewardess? This so-called music is driving me crazy." I told her I was sorry, but the plane was full. "If you've got to sing," she went on, leaning across the aisle and tapping the young man, "can't you give us one of the lovely old hymns or carols? After all, this is Christmas Day. Anything's better than this dreary drone of yours." Then, of course, the fat was in the fire. "Sorry, lady," said the singer. "Didn't you know? Christmas is out this year." "How can you say such a terrible thing?" said the lady. "Young people nowadays are so arrogant, so insolent. Oh, yes, I've found it in every place I've visited. And I've been right round the world, let me tell you." Mike really bristled then. I bet the lady somehow recalled for him a fussy mother or a bossy school-marm. "I've been around a bit too," he said. "I don't think young people are so arrogant. They're more honest, that's all. Come to that, I doubt if people on world package tours like yours ever actually see anything or meet anyone; not really. You don't get farther than the tourist guide, the standard sights, the Intercontinental Hotel." "All I'm asking for is a little peace and goodwill," said the lady huffily. "Isn't that what Christmas stands for?" At which point a professor-looking type in the next seat to the lady had to look up from the big book he was reading and put in his bit. "I'm sorry, madam," he said. "I don't care for the young man's music any more than you do, but I'm afraid he's right about Christmas." "Oh, I know there's a lot of commercialism of course," said the lady. "Believe me, I've seen it in shops everywhere from the Philippines to Singapore. I've come home loaded with silly presents for all my friends. My baggage is kilos overweight and it's costing me a fortune."

"It's not the commercialism that worries me," said the professor, his neatly trimmed black beard bobbing in the dim light, as he stabbed the air with a ball-point. "Good luck, I say, to the traders if they can make some money out of gullible tourists. No, it's not the commercialism. It's the sentimentality. I don't think Christmas is just harmlessly silly. I think it's positively dangerous." "Can I get any of you people a drink of something?" I interposed rather hastily. Politics or religion on an international flight are things to be avoided. "Anyway," I couldn't help adding, "I'm not a Christian myself, but I'd like to wish everyone a merry Christmas." Unfortunately, the professor hadn't finished yet—in fact he was just warming up. Laying aside his book and taking off his glasses, he turned to all and sundry. "When I say that the Christmas idea is dangerous," he began, as though delivering a lecture to a class of backward students, "I mean just exactly that."

"Well then, I wish you'd just exactly pipe down," said the American lady, now raring for a fight. But the professor was not easily deterred. As I moved up and down the plane, I could hear odd snatches as he went droning on. "The harsh world of reality . . . the myth of the Christ child, a combination of mystery religions, astrology and pagan fertility cults . . . beautiful in its way no doubt, but taking the human race out of the scientific age back into a fantasy world . . . primitive emotions, irrational reactions, wish fulfilment, ancient taboos and so forth and so forth." The American lady had given up the argument and was settled back in her seat with eyes closed and a determined look of Christian martyrdom on her face. Mike was still plaintively asking to be saved from himself in several different keys.

I was just trying to stop the professor in full flow by offering him a free Coca Cola, when we were all startled by a sharp cry from the back seat. I turned to find the young Palestinian girl writhing in pain. "Can you please help us?" said her husband desperately. "I think it's beginning." It was more than beginning. She had been enduring in silence as long as she could. Now the birth-pangs were upon her, and for us in the cabin crew it was the beginning, too, of the test of our lives. Oh, we had lectures during our training about dealing with every sort of emergency from birth to death. We had had some rudimentary medical instruction, coloured slides and all. It had all sounded very matter-of-fact and straightforward, one more item in a whole array of crises to be overcome. I hurriedly called the others. The first thing to settle was where it was all going to happen. Our own cramped galley where we served the food was impossibly cluttered and small. We couldn't easily carry her into the first class. The only thing was to clear the two or three back rows of seats, curtain them off with blankets, reverse a couple of rows and improvise a little delivery room right round her. As for drugs or instruments, we were not supposed to touch them without medical supervision. There must be a doctor somewhere among the passengers. There nearly always is. Anju hurried to the microphone to appeal to any doctor or nurse on board to come and help us, while I had the unenviable job of asking some twelve passengers in a packed economy class to give up their seats. Once they grasped what was up, they were all wonderfully co-operative and willing. We offered them our own jump seats and our previous reserved section. The Shepherd boys woke from their sleep. Everyone wanted to help. The thought of an immediate birth in mid-flight was exciting. The only exception was the professor. "Typical," he muttered, "utterly typical of that particular class of person. They should have stayed home where they were. The medical services in Israel are some of the best in the world." "Always remembering," said the American lady, "that their village was totally destroyed by those same Israelis, deliberately burned, their homes in ruins." "And why? Why?" shouted the professor, his face white with anger. "Because those same villagers one week before had pillaged and ravaged an Israeli settlement nearby, killing men, women and children. They asked for it. There is only one way such people will ever learn. By retaliation, retribution, swift, immediate and sure."

He was hurried down to the other end of the plane, out of sight, out of earshot, while Anju repeated her appeal for medical help, and we began to prepare hot water and towels. The husband, who told us his name was Jo Daoudi, stayed close to his wife, comforting and encouraging her. But nothing could hide the desperate anxiety on his face. "If only a doctor were here," he whispered to us. "They warned us it might be a very difficult birth."

The wife's sharp cries were becoming more and more insistent, and at shorter intervals. We had little doubt that Jo Daoudi was right. Suddenly I felt a tap on my shoulder. It was the young singer Mike from the Shepherd group. "Excuse me," he said. "You'd better keep out of here," I hissed, "we're crowded enough already." "No, but I've seen something. I've got to tell you. That professor fellow who was sitting here. I helped him carry his stuff. I could swear that one of his things was a medical bag. I asked him point blank if he was in medicine, but he refused to answer." "He's listed as Doctor on the passenger sheet," said Anju. "I checked." "But he can't be a medical doctor," I said, "otherwise he'd have offered his services." "Leave this to us," said the boy, "we'll get it out of him," and he vanished. The serious business had begun, and believe me it was serious. We stewardesses were hopelessly out of depth. Meanwhile general murmur had broken out in the plane, people arguing, some asking to help, offering advice, protesting. Anju jumped to the mike. "Please will you all resume your places," she said as calmly as she could manage. "There is so little room. There is no room here for anyone who is not qualified. We are doing the best we can. If any of you are accustomed to pray," she added, "please do so now, for us, and especially for this mother and her child." Then at last the professor arrived escorted, almost pushed by Mike. "Thank God," I cried. "Can you help us?" "He'd better," said Mike grimly, "or else. He's a doctor all right." "Thanks," I whispered. "Okay," he said as he turned back to his seat. "Anything to oblige. You never know, I might even revert to my chapel days and join the prayer squad." "You do that," I giggled (nerves of course). "You might even get saved from yourself."

Meanwhile Anju and the others were talking urgently to the doctor, catching him up with the situation so far. He was still protesting. "I'm not a practising doctor. It's years . . . since I've delivered a child. I'm in research. There must be someone else." "There's no-one else. You've just got to help us." "Show me your drug cabinet," he snorted. Then he went to work. I've never seen such skill or speed or precision. Yet all the time he was muttering, talking partly to himself, partly to us. "I'm a fool to be here. Try and help people like this, and what happens? Something goes wrong and you get sued for your pains. Doubt if my insurance covers an International flight." And then in the same breath, "Pass me that probe and for God's sake be quick about it. She's had about as much as she can take." "Thank God you're here, Doctor," Jo whispered. "How can we ever repay you?" "Don't talk to me about repaying." He'd snort again. "And don't forget, if your village was harmed, that was repayment in kind. The only kind of repaying you people will ever understand. Now, Stewardess, I need your help. If you are the one who suggested praying, let me tell you it doesn't work. A primitive fetish. This is better." Sweat was pouring down his face. The sweating abated a little, as the struggle for a life went on. The mother's courage was matched by his own. I realised that without him we would never have had an earthly chance. We'd have lost the child and probably the mother as well. It was no simple, ordinary birth. It required all the skill of a highly trained professional. Then at last it was over. Suddenly through the now silent cabin there rang out the sound of a baby's cry. I popped my head through the blanket curtains and had a quick word with the others, checked up on a few essential details, and then, with knees wobbling and my trained stewardess voice husky with strain, I went to the microphone and made an announcement. "Ladies and gentlemen," I said, "I'm happy to announce the safe arrival on this 'plane of a new passenger. It's a fine handsome boy. Mother and child seem to be doing well." And then as an even more breathless after-thought I added, "And on behalf of the Captain and crew, may I wish them and all of you an especially happy Christmas."

There were shouts, cheers, congratulations. Everybody started wishing one another a happy Christmas, the Shepherds at the back started up a version of 'Happy Birthday to you'. Drinks were ordered to celebrate, and the Captain arrived to announce that they were on the house, and to join in the general jubilation, not without a certain patronising air as though he had virtually delivered the baby himself. Then there were cries for the 'proud father' and after a lot of delay and a good deal of encouragement, Jo Daoudi appeared from behind the blanket curtain. Somebody requested a speech, but Jo was too dazed and shaken to produce more than beaming smiles. In all the excitement, we scarcely noticed that morning had come. We drew back the shields over the cabin windows, to let in brilliant sunshine above white, fleecy clouds. At last Jo found his voice, and made a little speech of thanks to those within earshot. "But we've forgotten the real hero of the day," he said. "The doctor, we'd never have done it without the doctor." Everyone seemed to have forgotten the doctor. Heads were turned, questions were asked. Where was the doctor? He wasn't still with the mother and child; he hadn't returned to his seat. The doctor seemed to have disappeared.

"I know where he is," said Mike suddenly. "He went into the washroom directly it was over, and I don't think he's come out again." Next moment Mike, who seldom wasted time turning words into action, was hammering on the locked door. "Doctor," he was shouting, "are you in there? Are you all right?" No answer! "Doctor! Please come on out. Everyone wants to see you." An angry voice from behind the door, "Leave me alone, can't you? I don't want to see anybody." The door remained bolted and shut. Finally Jo went to the door, knocked on it gently, and in a pleading voice said, "Doctor, we understand. You must be exhausted. But if we could just see you; if I could just see you to thank you in person, to shake you by the hand. After all, you've saved the life of my child, perhaps of my wife too." There was silence in the plane as the sun rose higher and the light became more brilliant. At last the door slowly opened and out came the professor. He was drawn and drained and looked grim. As he stood there, every head turned to see him, there was absolute silence for a moment, and then clapping broke out. Jo led the clapping louder than the rest. Then he took the professor by the arm and said, "Won't you come, Professor? My wife wants to thank you in person. Besides you must see the baby again. He's a beautiful boy." The professor pulled away angrily. "No thanks; and I wish you'd all leave me alone . . . I've done my duty. Isn't that enough? I'm pretty well done in." "Tell you the truth, I'm exhausted myself," said the American lady. "It's the most exciting experience of my whole trip. What a story it will make with the folks back in Esperance, Ohio. Could I take pictures of you all? They'll never believe me otherwise." Before we knew it she was flashing bulbs all over the place. This was the very last straw as far as the professor was concerned. Suddenly with a roar he knocked the camera out of the American's hand, just as she was about to take his picture. . . . "For God's sake," he shouted. "That's enough of this drooling sentimentality. I'm sick of it. Birth is a purely scientific phenomenon that takes place in our world hundreds of thousand of times a day. Far, far too often in my opinion. In the conditions most people live in, birth is not a cause for congratulation. It is an inconvenience to be prevented or avoided as often as possible, especially on crowded aeroplanes. Where is this child you make such a fuss about going to grow up? Probably in the Middle East, where he will learn to hate and to kill, if he does not get murdered first."

"Hold on there," chimed in Mike, ever ready to put his foot in it. "The world may be all you say it is. I've seen plenty to turn my stomach. All the same, I imagine that most of us are glad on the whole that somebody took the trouble to help us get born into it. Anyway," and he turned angrily on the professor, "is all this the reason why you were so uneager to help? You'd have never let it be known that you were a doctor; I don't believe you would have come forward to help at all if some of us hadn't dragged it out of you. Honestly, I saw what happened." He turned to some of us. "I believe he'd have just sat there and let mother and baby die if we hadn't pushed him into it." "Come to think of it, I believe that's true," said the American lady, thoroughly miffed at her broken camera. "I don't believe this doctor man, or whatever he is, would have lifted a finger to help if it had been left to him. I wouldn't imagine anyone could be so cold-bloodedly selfish, if I hadn't seen it with my own eyes."

"Is it only doctors then," said the professor, "who are supposed to be unselfish? You've been round the world, madam, taking your snapshots, seeking your little adventures to dazzle the folks back home. Have you ever answered the call to relieve misery or feed the hungry? And you," turning to Mike, "as you tour the world making your insane animal-like music, picking up dope, doing your thing, making an infernal nuisance of yourself, who are you to tell others their duty?"

By this time there was a fight likely to break out, when Jo Daoudi stepped in again. "Wait a minute," he said. "Let's postpone the war until after Christmas. You'll be waking the baby. Besides," he added, turning once more to the professor, "if this gentleman was reluctant to help, I'm sure there was a reason, a special reason. I think I understand it; we who come from Palestine, understand many things. I think you are Jewish, aren't you, Doctor? We are Palestinians. We have suffered as a race. We feel often we have been treated unjustly. Often we thirst for revenge, and what we call justice. Perhaps this gentleman and his people have suffered more. Could that be true in your case, sir?"

Silence!

"Only a few weeks ago," Jo went on, "we had a nice little home, a prosperous carpenter's trade in a village in Galilee. We were contented. Then the soldiers and the police came in. We were given one hour to evacuate everything. And then the whole village, houses, shops, our home and business, everything we left behind, were deliberately blown up by dynamite and set on fire."

"Because some of your people," said the professor, white with fury, "had been into a neighbouring kibbutz and murdered people, women and children who weren't given an hour to escape."

"Were you in that kibbutz?" said Jo gently.

"Not that one," said the professor more quietly. "I had the sense to get out some years ago. But I knew it all when I read it in the paper. It was as if I had been there."

"Tell us about it," said Jo. "It might help us all."

He started slowly, with pause and hesitation, and then the story gathered speed until it grew into a torrent, a torrent of hate.

Many years before, the professor had emigrated from somewhere in eastern Europe to Israel. He had joined a few others, and had formed a kibbutz somewhere in the north, close to the Lebanon border. Together they had irrigated the land, dynamited the rocks, made a wilderness into a garden, where they grew oranges and grapefruit and began to export worldwide. There he had met a Jewish girl. They shared the same ideals, the same hopes. They married and a child was born. They shared in the life of the community. They saw the desert blossom as the rose. They started schools, then a hospital. The professor continued his medical practice and study. Together with others he was instrumental in founding a small college. They had dreams of a university and a medical school. Then one night the blow fell. The terrorists came over the border from Lebanon. No warning, no reason that the professor knew at least. Houses were set on fire, people were dragged from their beds.

In a deathly hush, the whole plane heard the final scene. The professor and his wife, who was a trained nurse, went out to try in some way to help the wounded. Their son, aged four, ran from the home to follow them. Amid the shouting and confusion, another bomb suddenly exploded. The mother and the boy were in the place of the full blast. "I prayed that night, I prayed I tell you," he almost shouted, "as some of you prayed tonight. In my case, and in the case of my wife and child, it was no use. Neither was seen again. In due course I emigrated once more, I decided to go as far as I possibly could from the land I had called home. I ended up in Australia, where I have become involved in research in one of the universities. At times I feel that I have forgotten. I have become absorbed in a new life. I have friends, interests, a high degree of comfort and security. I live for the most part in peace and tranquillity. I sometimes travel to Europe or America to deliver lectures or carry out further medical research. The old life is dead and gone, until . . . until. . . .

"Until," said Jo, "people like us bring it all back again."

"I suppose I have never lost for one moment," said the professor, "the thirst for revenge. Not just public revenge; private revenge, personal revenge. Suddenly, last night, I saw my chance. As a doctor I realised what was happening, what probably might happen, if a difficult birth was attempted on this plane. I could picture it all. And I . . . I . . ." he said with a kind of choking sob, "all I needed to do was to sit quiet in my seat, to do nothing, say nothing, and the most perfect, personal revenge might be mine. Another mother, another child, to pay for the lives of my own."

There was a long, long silence. Everyone was caught up in the drama.

Suddenly, the Captain's voice came through on the loud-speaker. He was doing his stuff, poor fellow, but right at that moment he sounded more pompous and inappropriate than ever.

"Good morning, ladies and gentlemen. A merry Christmas to all of you. We are now approaching London. But it may be some little time before we land. The sky over London is very thick and overcast. There are several 'planes stacked up here waiting to go down through the hole in the sock, as we say. We'll have to take our turn."

Actually it broke the strain and the tension, and people were relieved to talk normally again. "Fog over London," said someone. "Typical." "It looks so white and fleecy," said the American lady, "you feel you could bounce on it." "Why not have a go?" said Mike encouragingly. "You might land somewhere plop down the chimney. Christmas angel."

By this time we were busy again with orange juice and coffee. Anju was staying with the mother and baby. Jo had gone behind the curtain screen to join them. We were all suddenly bright and relieved. The Christmas spirit was catching on. Mike and his friends seemed to be in a huddle composing a song.

Then suddenly it happened. We started to make our descent. What had been bright and brilliant sunshine a moment before became swirling cloud and thick fog. The plane shuddered a little and we were all plunged in almost total darkness. We were helping people back to their seats, when Anju suddenly, without warning, lowered the improvised curtain of rugs that we had put up to shelter the emergency birth. The curtain fell away and. . . .

I don't know what others saw. I can't tell you what was really there. All I know is that, for me, there under a single light, in the darkened plane, there shone out what I had so often seen in paintings, a Nativity scene. The mother seated, the child in her arms, with Jo standing just behind. It was every Christmas card, every carol, suddenly alive before us. Then, as the plane steadied again and we continued circling around in the fog, yet another extraordinary happening seemed to be taking place. Was I dreaming or was it an emotional reaction, a light-headedness after the crisis of the night? Whatever it was, others felt it too. Several passengers stood up in their seats, looking at the mother and child, and, each in his own way, according to his custom, making some kind of obeisance, some stretching out a hand, some touching their foreheads, some even kneeling and making the sign of the cross in the half-light as they gazed at the purity and wonder of the scene.

If, for me, a take-off feels like drama, a landing is more like a symphony. The changes in the pitch of the engine, the altered air-pressures, the pulsating throbs and rhythms. This time it seemed all to be mixed up with other music. I could swear some kind of heavenly chorus had somehow joined in the act. Or was it the Shepherds? Led of course by Mike, they had concocted a sort of pop-calypso carol with which to glorify the occasion. More and more of the passengers were turning to look. Then even two or three first-class passengers came through to join in. They didn't exactly look like the wise men of tradition, but they moved with a certain ponderous dignity that made you feel they had probably been riding on camels from some mysterious other land. Anyway they made their way back, the Arab oil sheikh, the large trade-union leader, the African notable in a gorgeous native costume. They weren't exactly bearing gifts, but they made you think that, given the chance, they could have afforded some fairly costly ones.

"May I have your attention please," came the Captain's voice through the public address system. "I'm glad to tell you that we now have clearance for landing. Will you all resume your seats, and be sure your seat-belts are fastened? It may be a bit bumpy."

"Good old London, here we come," said someone.

"Hey, Doctor," said Mike. "Welcome to London. You haven't been back to see the baby yet."

"Not me," said the doctor; but not defiant this time. Just humble. "Not me."

"Of course you must go," said Mike persuasively. "They might still need you, you know."

"No, I tell you, I can't."

"Why are you talking so daft? It was with you Jewish people the whole thing started, wasn't it."

And then Mike sang quietly and lovingly, same as he must have done way back in Wales.

"The Lord looked down from His starry throne,
And He saw His children lost and alone,
And He knew they'd hate and kill and mock,
So He came down through the hole in the sock."

The 'plane had come to a standstill. "Come on, Doc," said Mike. "Let's go."

Slowly they went back together. Everyone stayed in their places watching them. The Nativity scene was still there, frozen, just as in the Christmas cards. But as Mike and the doctor took their place standing close to it all, Jo stepped forward. He took the doctor by the hand and drew him very close. For a moment or two they stood together, side by side, looking down at the mother and child. Jo had his arm round the doctor's shoulder.

Then, can you believe it, the Captain himself came through the 'plane and joined them. He was all dressed up in his full regalia, and he looked pretty gorgeous. He had a gift in his hand. It was in the form of a scroll, which he solemnly handed to Jo. "By International custom," he said, in his rich, fruity Captain's voice, "anyone born on an International flight gets a free passage on the airline for the rest of his life."

My Christian doctrine is a bit mixed up, but it sounded sort of appropriate. "A free passage for the rest of his life."

The plane door began to open. "Wake up in there," came a
voice. "We hear you've an emergency on board."

An immigration official climbed in, followed by an ambu-
lance man in a white coat.

"Hello, you people," said the official. "Happy Christmas!"
Then he stopped in his tracks, taking in the scene.

"My God!" he said, in a kind of awed whisper.

"That's right," I said.

Baboushka

There once lived deep in the heart of Russia an old peasant woman whose name was Baboushka. Baboushka lived by herself yet she was happy and wanted for nothing. She had a fine cabin made of logs cut from the best fir trees in the forest, and a good garden in which to grow vegetables. "I am a fortunate woman," Baboushka would say to herself. "Have I not food in the cupboard and a good fire in the big black stove." Her hospitality was known throughout the forest where she lived, for when a tired traveller passed by the old woman would call, "Friend, stop and rest in my cabin," and indeed they would.

One day, at the time when Mother Snow covers the great forests with her white mantle and Father Frost goes dancing from tree to tree decorating the branches with glittering icicles, old Babouskha was outside, busily clearing away the snow from her path, when three travellers came up to her gate. They were richly dressed in fine furs and each one carried a leather bag.

"Good day, Mother," they called.

"Good day to you, gentlemen," replied Babouskha, a little breathless, for clearing snow is no easy task for an old woman. "Can I help you?" asked Baboushka.

"Indeed you can, good Mother," said the first stranger, "for we have travelled far and have need of food and warm beds to sleep in."

"Then come inside," she answered. "I have black bread made this very morning and hot tea on the stove. As for beds, there is only one, for I live on my own, but it's large enough for three."

When the three travellers had eaten and drunk all they could so that their stomachs no longer felt empty, they settled down in the old woman's bed, thanked her for her kindness and went to sleep. While the travellers slept Baboushka baked more black bread for the next day. But as she baked, the more she thought about the three strangers. "Is it not so," thought Baboushka to herself, "that all good men sleep by night and travel by day? When they rise I shall ask them why they travel so."

As Mother Evening came creeping over the forest, spreading her grey veil behind her, the three travellers awoke and started to make ready to depart.

"Kind sirs," Baboushka said, "why is it that you journey by night and sleep by day? For surely it is hard to find your way in the darkness of the night."

"Good Mother," said the first man, "we are three Kings who have travelled far from the lands of the East."

"We search for the Christ Child," said the second King. "Many years we have been waiting for a mighty star to appear in the heavens and now it has. For it is told that beneath that star the Christ Child will be born. It will guide all who wish to pay homage to the new-born child."

"We travel by night," said the third King, "so that we may follow the star. Each of us carries a gift to give the Christ Child. The first King gold, the second King myrrh, and I take frankincense."

"Oh, how I would like to go with you," said Baboushka, in wonderment at what the three Kings had told her. "I have no rich things to give but I could take my black bread, for they say it is the finest in the forest."

"Then come, good Mother," replied the first King, "but you must follow us now, or we shall lose sight of the star."

"That is impossible," cried poor Baboushka, "for I must first clean my cabin and see that all is put away. Can you not wait for me just a little longer?"

The Kings shook their heads sadly, saying that they could

not lose a moment longer, but told the old woman to hurry her work and follow after them. This Baboushka said she would do, and bidding the Kings goodbye started to clean her cabin.

When at last Baboushka had finished her work, she wrapped her great winter cloak around herself and taking her black bread opened the door of her cabin. But as old Baboushka looked up into the night sky to find the great star, she felt her heart break. For the star had gone. Baboushka had taken so long to clean her cabin that night had given way to dawn. Even the Kings' tracks had been covered up by the newly fallen snow.

"How silly I was to see to my home, I should have left with the Kings," sobbed the old woman. "No matter, I shall travel on. Surely there must be someone who has seen the Kings. They will tell me which way they went and I will follow." And so Baboushka trudged through the snow asking all she met, "Have you seen three Kings? Which way were they going?" but each answer was the same: "No."

Days turned into weeks and weeks turned into months, while Baboushka, footsore, tired and hungry, looked in vain for the Christ Child. After many months Baboushka met a traveller sitting by the roadside.

"Have you seen three Kings who go to see the Christ Child?" asked Baboushka.

"Three Kings I have not seen, old woman," said the traveller, "but I have been told of a child who will one day be King. He was born not far from here; they call the town Bethlehem. But stay awhile, you look too ill to travel on, old woman."

"I must," said Baboushka, "I have travelled far and cannot stop now that I am so near the Christ Child's birthplace."

At last Baboushka came to Bethlehem.

"Where is the one they call the Christ Child?" she inquired of a woman washing at a well.

"If you believe that story," laughed the woman, "you will believe anything. Well, if you want to know, the Child and the family have gone. They stayed in a stable; it's at the top of that hill. Look, you can see it from where we are standing."

Baboushka thanked the woman and made her way up the hill to the stable. Inside Baboushka found it empty, except for one donkey and an ass, who brayed and snorted in greeting.

"Ah me," sighed Baboushka, "I am too late, but I shall lay my black bread in the manger, then the Christ Child will know I came. I shall sleep here for the night and start home in the morning. Come, donkey and ass, we shall sleep side by side tonight, for it is cold outside."

Soon Baboushka fell into a deep sleep only to be awakened by a beautiful golden light, which came from the far corner of the stable.

"Baboushka, Baboushka, I am here. Come rise and greet me," said a child's voice.

"Who are you?" cried Baboushka in fright.

"Do you not know, have you not been looking for me? I am the one they call the Christ Child."

"O Child, I have waited so long to see you."

"Then walk into my light, Baboushka, and let us hold hands," said the voice softly.

And Baboushka did so.

The next day they found old Baboushka dead, curled up on the straw, with only the donkey and ass to watch over her.

But that is not quite the end of my story. For every Christmas Eve children all over Russia hang up their stockings in the hope that they will be full in the morning. And so they are, with toys and games, and right at the bottom in coloured paper is a piece of black bread. The old ones who know nod their heads and say Mother Christmas has been there. "See, Baboushka has left some black bread. Just as she did for the Christ Child all those years ago."

The Christmas Dinner of Silas Squeer

You might say Silas Squeer was a misfit. To see him tramping the streets in his threadbare, discoloured overcoat, his down-at-heel shoes, his old and rumpled hat jammed tight on his head, you would not think that he came from a background of privilege. Here, you would have said, is a downtrodden man. Here is a man for whom society has not cared and does not care. He obviously has not enough—neither warm clothes to keep out the wind's edge, nor good shoes to keep out the wet, nor good warm food inside to lift his spirit and cheer him through a winter's day.

And all the sorry things you felt for Silas Squeer as he passed you in the street would make you feel bitter against the society which tolerated such a state of affairs. And doubly so at Christmas time. For at Christmas, that time of warmth and cheer, when the shop windows glow gaily, when people everywhere are spending their money freely, expectation of largesse is in the air. Indeed, the snowflakes that floated down this Christmas Eve were like the sprinkling of gifts that seemed to fill the atmosphere.

That is, everywhere except in the soul and in the neighbourhood of Silas Squeer. For him, each lighted window was a mockery. The warm glow of lights through the curtains, with their suggestion of a merry fire inside and cheerful company sitting round a loaded table, emphasized the loneliness and coldness of his existence. The whole festive season was a bitter contrast to the soul of Silas Squeer. Where fairy lights twinkled on Christmas trees, blackness filled his heart. Carol singers in cheerful voices intoning "Tidings of comfort and joy, comfort and joy" underlined for him the absence of comfort in his life, the non-existence and improbability of there ever being joy.

Now what vicious act of society had done these sad things to Silas Squeer? Where had the system failed, that he was not properly cared for in a state allocating much wealth to the welfare of its citizens? What form had he not filled in that happiness should thus by-pass him?

Well, the strange truth was, as it so often is in life, that if the story were told by someone else other than Silas Squeer, they might well have said that he had only himself to blame. If you asked him, he could explain how every man's hand was turned against him. Yet it might be that the Recording Angel, noting down the facts of his life—or even, in a really well-organized state, some efficient civil servant keeping check on each individual in a computer programme—would state that he had been born to a well-to-do family; he had been to the best schools and had been trained to hold down a lucrative post anywhere in the world.

Indeed, his various brothers and sisters had managed along very happily. Even now, they were sitting with their well-clothed and educated children and wives, enjoying the material and possibly even something of the spiritual pleasures that go with Christmas. While Silas Squeer sauntered unhappily through the streets, surrounded by Christmas yet not part of it. Indeed, signs of joy and revelry angered him. Undernourished, weary and cold as he was, a pink flush of anger came to his cheeks as he heard carollers singing. He cursed under his breath as cheerful people made their way home gaily laughing and chatting, while if someone had been unwise enough to wish him a "Merry Christmas" in friendly tones, there is no doubt they would have been shocked at the tone and venom of his response. But happily the normal decencies prevented any passer-by in a big city from making any greeting to the sad bundle that was Silas Squeer, and he was able to go his way unmolested, nursing jealously his own bitternesses and miseries to himself, indulging in them as happily as others do in song and banter at the Christmas season.

So Christmas night passed, as Silas Squeer paced the chilly streets. He knew the places he could huddle in the shadow of old buildings where the wind did not reach him so keenly, where dozing was possible. He sat and nursed his grievances against mankind, and thought malevolently of all those who had wronged him throughout his life.

Around midnight he was disturbed by revellers and by people going to and from midnight services. He cursed them as they troubled his doze. Again, early in the morning, simple people going to church disturbed him. "Fools!" he growled to himself. Hadn't they got comfortable beds? As for filing into a chilly church . . . he had got over all superstition long since.

So dawned Christmas Day. Not doubtfully and greyly, but brightly and crisply. As the day wore on, there came a point when the horizon of Silas Squeer was dominated by one thought—Christmas dinner. For him there became nothing else in life but the thought of sitting down in a warm room to a succulent dish of hot food. No other thought could come into his focus—his one supreme fixation was—and heaven knows, understandably enough—Christmas dinner; the prospect of it; how to get it; what in the whole of heaven and earth could be done to obtain this, the ultimate, the highest thing that life could offer.

At Joe's Place, a poor man could be sure of a good hot meal and the comfort of a good hot, steamy atmosphere while he ate it. Joe's food was filling and the prices were absurdly cheap. Absurdly . . . but the absurd thing for Silas Squeer was even to think of buying a meal, however low the price. For he had nothing; he did not even know where to go to borrow; and in his depressed state he had not the courage to steal.

Just the same, though, without the prospect of participating in the joys of the interior of Joe's Place, Silas Squeer propelled himself on his worn-out shoes towards its exterior. He glanced in through the steamy window; that steam meant inside it was warm, inside there was fellowship, inside there were delicious smells and hot cups of tea.

Yes, inside, those sybaritic joys; and outside, the frosty morning, the rising sun shedding only its light and no warmth, and the forlorn figure of Silas Squeer peering in through the window at the notice that read:

Joe's Place
SPECIAL CHRISTMAS DINNER
Turkey
Potatoes
Cabbage
Plum Pudding
Cup of Tea

HAPPY CHRISTMAS TO ALL!

Ah, those mocking words, Happy Christmas to All. All, that is, save Silas Squeer for whom there was no ration of happiness, no allocation of joy.

Knowing he had no money, he swung away from the window, passing a hand across his eyes to wipe away a few falling tears. God, how could a man be so mistreated, so forsaken, so neglected—and on Christmas Day? Not a friend anywhere. No one to care, no one to help.

Christmas—yes, fine for those fat people with money in their pockets. Fine for his brothers and sisters, cosy in their homes—but they lived in different worlds and he didn't intend to take a step towards them until they took one towards him. Perhaps, when next day's papers reported his death from undernourishment and exposure, they would feel sorry for him . . . too late. He revelled for a moment in the thought of their discomfiture, their remorse.

Christmas—what did it all add up to anyway? Christmas—what was all the celebration about? Just a racket to sell more things. Just an excuse to eat and drink too much. How had it all started? It had started long ago—let's see, something to do with a child being born, a child in a stable somewhere. It was all very long ago and very disconnected with the present.

Oh yes, the child was supposed to be the Son of God; indeed, some said he was God, born on earth. Well, good luck to Him. Even God hadn't been able to do much with this sorry world; it was in a mess then, it was in a mess today, and Silas Squeer didn't see any prospect of its doing anything except get into a worse mess. Meanwhile, people were eating, drinking and making merry, for tomorrow we die. . . .

Tomorrow we die. Silas Squeer shivered a little and pulled his coat a little closer round him. He didn't want to die. It might be a wretched world but he wanted to live.

God. What had he got to do with all this? One thing, thank heaven, we'd all got over all these old superstitions like belief in God and all that sentimental rot. We all knew today that it was an economic world we lived in; the economic factor governed everything—and especially the life of Silas Squeer.

Happiness for him was the price of Joe's Christmas dinner. All joy, all comfort, all the solace in this world could offer was, for him, the good dinner with a cup of hot tea reaching down and warming to his toes, the steamy warm heat and the fellowship of Joe's Place—and for only a few coins.

Silas Squeer thought of all the plenty he'd enjoyed in the early days, how money had meant nothing to him them. And today all happiness was wrapped up in somehow obtaining enough for Joe's Christmas dinner.

Friends, that was it! One had to have friends. That was the way to have money. But Silas Squeer sobbed a bitter tear as he thought how he had no friends. True, many had said it was his fault that he had no friends, but, well, his pride wasn't going to let him go back snivelling and whining and apologizing to people. Besides, after all these years, it was doubtful if they would even remember him or take him into their homes. "It's some man at the door, Ma'am." "Oh, we can't see anyone today—it's Christmas Day."

Christmas Day. Oh the bleakness of it! He had no friends. He had no money. He had no home. He had, worst of all, no prospect of Christmas dinner. "It's not much to ask from life, just dinner on Christmas Day," he murmured miserably.

A ray of light shining in a dirty puddle at his feet impacted on his eye. He looked up to the sky. There the sun was shining, smiling, as it were, out of a blue sky down on him. In spite of himself, he could not help but feel momentarily cheered. The suggestion of a grin, an unwonted sight on Silas' face, troubled it for an instant.

That old sun was smiling, it looked happy and hopeful. But then it didn't need money. It wasn't tied to this gloomy earth with its limitations and bonds. It was free—free as the wind. "The best things in life are free"—the line of a tune from his youth flashed into his mind, and the grin (if one could call the temporary twisting of his thin mouth a grin) flew from his face. He was up against the problem again, the reality of life—where to find the money.

But that glance upwards had started a new train of thought. The sun in the heavens: God's in His heaven. But there is no God. But there might be. No, there isn't. Well, if there was, He might help. Who knows, there might be one and He might help. He was supposed to, especially poor people. Well, whether he believed it or not, it was worth trying.

With an effort, Silas Squeer turned his thinking towards this new problem of God. It was a bitter moment in his life when he decided he would pray. Not that he thought it could help, but he'd do it. It was a hard decision, because it meant throwing himself on to the mercy of a Goodness somewhere, he who had believed all his life there was no goodness, in men or elsewhere.

We will not go into the silent prayer that Silas Squeer thought, quite momentarily, looking up into the sun. In a moment it was all over, there was nothing to mark what had happened. No one saw; nothing had changed.

But there came a thought into the mind of Silas Squeer— "Bob Barkettle". Why, yes—Bob Barkettle. That name out of the past. It was years—maybe twenty years—since he'd last thought of or been in touch with Bob. They'd been at school together, close friends in their youth. Then Bob had gone out to Africa. Their ways had parted. They had never written to each other. Which meant that Bob wouldn't know of all that had befallen Silas; he wouldn't know he wasn't a respectable, well-fed member of society. He would of course lend him the money, he might even lend him more. Steady, no point in getting hysterical, he'd ask for just enough for Christmas dinner.

Now, how to track down Bob? He saw a phone booth. He went to it and started to look in the directory. As he did so, the doubts came flooding back. Bob Barkettle was dead. He was still in Africa. He wouldn't remember Silas. Then, as he read down through Barff, Barfinch, Barham, there he saw "Barkettle, R. G. X."—yes, that was Bob, there wouldn't be two Robert George Xerxes Barkettles. An exclusive address, yes, that used to be his parents' home. Silas felt his pulse throbbing. He was definitely onto something. That prayer—it might have had something to do with it. . . .

As he memorised the number, he felt automatically in his pocket for change. And as he did so, he realized the futility of it—for of course he had no change. He had nothing. The whole thing was a lighthearted mirage sent to torture him, as men dying of thirst are tortured in the desert. And he was in an asphalt and concrete desert.

But wait. Down among the old papers and odds and ends in his pocket he had felt something hard, something that moved, that felt like it might be money. Excitedly, he dived deep into his pocket. It was money!

The pockets of Silas Squeer reflected the mess and confusion of his life; but in the mercy of providence among the garbage remained something useful. His eyes glistened as he saw them. More than coins, they were a talisman, a token that he was not deserted, that life was going to do him a good turn at last, a proof that goodness and mercy still existed—the promise of a new sort of life. It was a miracle.

He read the number carefully again, gingerly inserted his precious coins and dialled. He waited. He could hear the clicks and grunts as the fantastic machinery, housed on eight floors of a building somewhere, obeyed, like a genii, his wishes.

Well, we will pull aside now from that phone booth, and let the next few unhappy moments of Silas Squeer's life pass without too closely watching his misery. For, sad to tell, there was no reply. He redialled, but each time the same result—only the monotony of the dialling tone.

Then it was that the unhappy Silas Squeer spotted a little notice, modestly stuck to the old instructions, announcing that the price of local calls had gone up. So there he was, caught by the rising tide of inflation, pipped by a coin. His soaring spirits were dashed down. Disillusion hit him. Why had he hoped so much? What a fool. Surely the years, if they'd taught him nothing else, had shown him that the one thing to do was never to expect too much. Only so could a man avoid disappointment.

Of course he wouldn't get through. If he had, of course, Bob Barkettle wouldn't be there. He ought to have known it from the first and not built up his hopes like a naïve fool. As for that notion that some remote God in some remote corner of the heavens was aiding him—aiding him personally—well, that was clearly as crazy as it could be. (a) There was no God. (b) If there was, it was pretty unlikely He would bother Himself with individuals. (c) The last person He would interest Himself in would be Silas Squeer.

So thinking, Silas Squeer turned to leave. At that moment his eye spied on the floor of the phone box a woman's purse. He picked

it up. There was money inside it—notes as well as silver. Much
more than he needed for Christmas dinner!

Now Silas Squeer's heart should have jumped for joy. Yet he
felt strangely troubled by his sudden possession. What was he to
do? He held in his hand the money he so much wanted. Yet it
wasn't his. Somehow the thought of that God, if there was one,
must have persisted in his subconscious. It was as if he felt some
great omnipotent eye drilling through his spine, watching the
movements within his heart and brain as the unhappy Silas Squeer
decided what he should do with that which he so eagerly sought, yet
which now lay in his hand as an embarrassment.

The strange and perhaps rather wonderful thing is that our
friend Silas Squeer, down in the depths though he was, decided
that his gains, though so providentially provided, were ill-gotten.
And though he had no love of policemen, he determined he would
make his way to the nearest police station and turn in the purse, a
decision that takes some making, especially when you're hungry,
when it's Christmas Day and you desperately long for some
Christmas dinner.

As he moved away from the phone booth, a shiny, expensive
car pulled up at the kerb, a chauffeur jumped out and a large, smart
woman came quickly over towards him. She looked worried.
She went to the booth, looked around and turned round,
perplexed.

Silas then realized she was looking for the purse. He went over to her: "Were you looking for this?"

"Oh, yes, thank you so much. I was so concerned. Not so much the money as an address in there . . . sentimental reasons. I'd promised my husband . . . he's been very ill . . . but thank you—thank you so very much." Relief dawned on her face and she smiled at him.

Remains of his manners returned to Silas, and he bowed stiffly and murmured, "Nothing, madam. Glad to oblige."

"I should like to reward you," she said. "You don't know what this means to me. Do tell me your name."

"Squeer," replied Silas.

"Not Silas Squeer?" she said, astonished.

"Yes," said Silas, equally amazed that anyone should know his name. "The very same."

"But you're the man I'm looking for. My husband, Bob Barkettle, you know, the financier, has been seriously ill. He's been asking for you. He remembers you so well from your boyhood days . . . Said you set his feet on the path to success . . . Says he'd do anything to see you again. I'd found an old address . . . was trying to find you. . . ."

As they cut swiftly along the empty streets in the expensive car driven by the smart chauffeur to the imposing house where Bob Barkettle lay ill, Mrs. Barkettle recalled for Silas the years that lay between his last meeting with Bob.

But strangely all that Silas Squeer could think of, in between occasional diversionary thoughts of turkey, plum pudding and other delicacies that were each moment growing nearer, was that there must be Someone somewhere who did care; that the Someone would always go on caring.